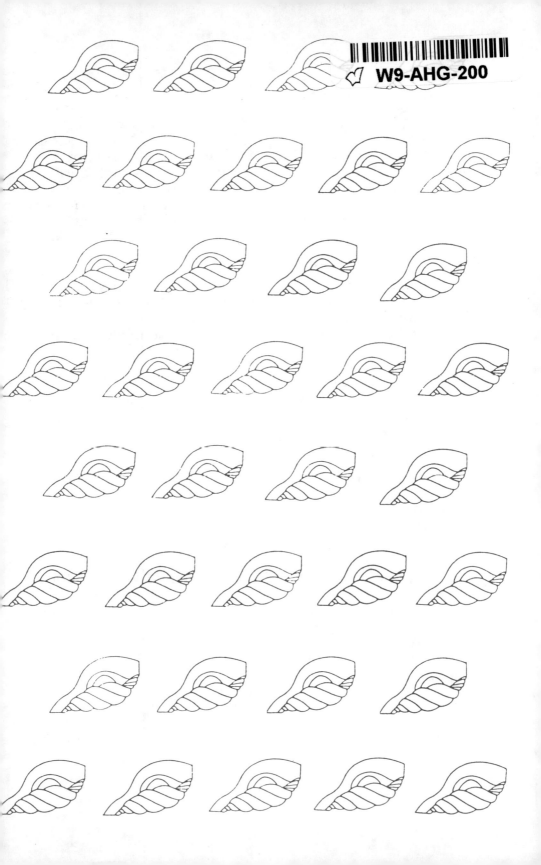

Our history is a sense of place, bound by those elements that do not change: deep forests, rich earth, ribboned quartz beaches spawned by an unceasing Gulf. This place...barrier islands, a vast bay, crooked bayous, a siren's song of ancient shores, a promise of magical days and unending nights...Okaloosa, beckons.

Responding, came the noble hunters — Indians before recorded time, wandering hunters...Weeden Island cultures, Temple Mound builders, Creek, Choctaws, Euchees...each succession archiving a collective past, tracking coastal waters and pristine shores.

Responding, came the fabled pirates, answering the mystical lure, the whispering winds...Captain Billy Bowlegs, in search of hidden coves and safe harbors, burying his treasure, hidden yet.

Responding, came the Scotch-Irish settlers, seeking the promises of freedom and abundance, founding churches, schools, and villages. Civil war interrupted. But still responding, came new generations, flourishing, nurtured by sun-drenched days, Spanish moss-cooled breezes, and ceaseless aqua seas.

Each people, following the past, shaped itself on the elements...forming the northern county seat around rich fertile lands and political realities. Offering the sweet, deep forests as a paradox to the soaring, silver jets, releasing the southern sand-strewn beaches to fishing villages and entranced visitors. These are the granules of our past. This is .....

The Sugar Beach

Virginia Glynn Barr

Sugar Beach

A Cookbook
by
The Junior League
Fort Walton Beach, Florida

The purpose of the Junior League of Fort Walton Beach is exclusively educational and charitable and is to promote voluntarism; to develop the potential of its members for voluntary participation in community affairs; and to demonstrate the effectiveness of trained volunteers.

Your purpose of *Sugar Beach* will benefit the community by helping support the following volunteer projects of the Junior League of Fort Walton Beach.

F.O.C.U.S. CENTER
Families of **O**kaloosa **C**ounty **U**nderstanding **S**cience
A hands-on discovery center for children and adults.

CHILD CLOTHING
A project to provide new school clothing
to underprivileged students.

SPEECH AND HEARING CLINIC
Provides full service evaluation and therapy for
speech, language and hearing disorders for all ages.

OKALOOSA WALTON COMMUNITY COLLEGE SCHOLARSHIP
An endowment that provides an annual scholarship
to an outstanding female student with financial need.

SAFE AT HOME ALONE
BUCKLE BEAR
Programs to educate pre-school and elementary
school students on safety procedures to follow when
adult supervision is not available.

First Edition
First Printing: 15,000 books
Second Printing: 15,000 books
Third Printing: 10,000 books

Copies of **Sugar Beach** may be obtained from the Junior League Headquarters in c/o:

Sugar Beach
Post Office Box 24
Fort Walton Beach, Florida 32549

ISBN: 0-961356-0-0

Printed in the USA by
WIMMER BROTHERS
A Wimmer Company
Memphis • Dallas • San Antonio

TABLE OF CONTENTS

— indicates Microwave

PRESENT COOKBOOK COMMITTEE
CO-CHAIRMAN
Sally Reagan   Sandy Trammell

MARKETING CHAIRMAN
Mitzi Henley

COMMITTEE
Cindy Adams   Lynn Kinlaw
Carin Kaelin   Sherri Scheer
Rhonda Watson

ORIGINAL COOKBOOK COMMITTEE
Chairman   Assistant Chairman
Elaine McLaughlin Stewart   Louise Burris

COOKBOOK COMMITTEE
Virginia Glynn Barr
Linda Carr   Anne Johnston

TESTING AND TASTING CHAIRMAN
Dixie Aftonomos   Brenda Lloyd
Lou Baughman   Caroline Maney
Liz Cavanah   Dinah Remington
Tisha Fleet   Suzanne Seemann
Elizabeth Gonzales   Christine Watson
Susan Lee   Pam White

MARKETING CHAIRMEN
Gail Bailey   Connie Lee

EDITING CHAIRMAN
Ellen Deckert

OFFICE MANAGER   TREASURER
Brenda Angel   Champee Kemp

SPECIAL ASSISTANCE
Jo Ann Kerr   Sandy Walker

SUGAR BEACH
COMMITTEE CHAIRMAN
1984	Elaine McLaughlin Stewart
1985	Louise Burris
1986	Carol DeBolt
1987	Marilyn Ankeney and Martha Bayer
1988	Marilyn Ankeney
1989	Sally Reagan
1990	Sally Reagan and Sandy Trammell

Sugar Beach is a collection of 400 recipes that were selected from over 1,800 recipes submitted and thoroughly tested. We are grateful to all who helped in the production of this book and wish to offer a special thank-you to all Junior League members, their families and friends who have contributed their recipes, their support and creative ideas.

Appetizers & Beverages

Appetizers

Beverages

Appetizer Croissants
Yield: 6½ dozen

1 cup	butter (do not use margarine)
2 cups	small curd cottage cheese
2 cups	flour
2 (3 ounce) packages	cream cheese with chives

Beat butter and cottage cheese together. Stir in flour. Divide into four balls and chill. Roll each ball out into a pie shape and cut into 16 wedges. Place a small amount of cream cheese on each wedge and roll up as crescents. Bake at 350 degrees F. for 30 minutes or until brown. Serve warm.

Aloha Fruit Dip
Yield: 2 cups

2 (3 ounce) packages	cream cheese, softened
⅔ cup	pineapple preserves
2 tablespoons	milk
1 teaspoon	lemon peel, finely shredded
4 teaspoons	lemon juice
1 cup	heavy whipping cream

Blend cream cheese and preserves. Stir in milk, lemon peel and lemon juice. Whip cream until soft peaks form. Fold into cream cheese mixture. Cover and chill. Serve with assorted fruit.

Jan Omley

Chutney Cheese Spread

1 (8 ounce) package	cream cheese
1 cup	chutney, chop large pieces
¼ teaspoon	dry mustard
1 teaspoon	curry powder
½ cup	pecans, chopped
	grated coconut

Combine all ingredients except coconut. Chill overnight. Form into a ball, roll in coconut and serve with crackers.

Linda Scoville

Creamy Orange Snaps   *Yield: 2 cups*

1 (11 ounce) can	mandarin oranges, drained
1 (8 ounce) container	whipped cream cheese
	powdered sugar to taste
	ginger snaps

Chop oranges and fold into cream cheese. Add sugar. If mixture is too stiff, add a small amount of juice from oranges. Serve with ginger snaps.

Jacque Hale

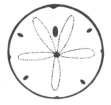

Party Pineapple   *Yield: 2 cups*

1 (16 ounce) can	fruit cocktail, drained and crushed
1 (8 ounce) package	cream cheese, softened
2 tablespoons	green onion tops, minced
2 tablespoons	mayonnaise
4 slices	bacon, cooked and crumbled
1 medium	pineapple
	parsley
	party rye bread

Combine first 5 ingredients, mix well and chill. Cutting lengthwise, remove 1/3 of the pineapple and scoop out pulp, leaving a 1/2 inch shell. Spoon cream cheese mixture into shell. Garnish with parsley and serve with party-size slices of rye bread.

Mary Lou Frederick

Strawberry Cheese Ring

2 cups	Cheddar cheese, grated
1 cup	nuts, chopped
1 cup	mayonnaise
1 small	onion, grated
dash	cayenne
dash	black pepper
	strawberry preserves

Mix all ingredients except preserves and mold into a ring. Chill in refrigerator. When ready to serve, fill center of ring with strawberry preserves. Serve with crackers.

Rhonda Mead

Kahlua Fruit Dip   *Yield: 4 cups*

Wonderful with apple and pear slices!

1 (8 ounce)	package cream cheese
1 (8 ounce) carton	whipped topping
¾ cup	light brown sugar
⅓ cup	Kahlua
1 cup	sour cream
1 (3 ounce) package	unsalted peanuts, finely chopped

Blend together cream cheese and whipped cream. Add sugar and Kahlua. Mix well. Add sour cream and peanuts. Refrigerate one or two days before serving. Serve with fresh fruit.

Lynne Handsel

Beefy Cheese Ball

¼-½ pound	beef stick
1 tablespoon	onion, finely chopped
16	green olives, sliced
½ teaspoon	Worcestershire sauce
1 tablespoon	mayonnaise
1 (8 ounce) package	cream cheese
	parsley

Grate beef stick; set aside 1 cup of meat. Mix remaining meat with all other ingredients except parsley. Form into a ball and roll in the remaining cup of grated meat and parsley. Serve with crackers.

Cindy McLaughlin

Beach Party Cheese Ball

Yield: 4 cups

2 (8 ounce) packages	cream cheese, softened
2 cups	sharp Cheddar cheese, shredded
1 tablespoon	pimento, chopped
1 tablespoon	green pepper, chopped
1 tablespoon	onion, finely chopped
1 tablespoon	Worcestershire sauce
1 teaspoon	lemon juice
¼ teaspoon	garlic powder
dash	cayenne
dash	salt
	pecans, finely chopped

Combine cream cheese and Cheddar cheese, mixing until well blended. Add remaining ingredients and chill. Shape into ball and roll in chopped pecans.

Alice Calhoun

Bacon Wraps

Serves: 10-12

A strange combination that tastes divine!

1 (8 ounce) package　dry pitted prunes
1 pound　bacon

Cut each prune in half and cut each strip of bacon in half. Wrap each strip of bacon around a prune. Secure with a wooden pick and broil until bacon is browned. Serve warm.

Virginia Glynn Barr

Rye Snacks

Yield: 2 dozen

⅓ cup　mayonnaise
¼ cup　Romano or Parmesan
　　　　cheese, grated
2 tablespoons　dried onion, minced
dash　Worcestershire sauce
　　　　salt and pepper to taste
　　　　rye party rounds

Combine all ingredients. Spread on rye party rounds or slices of rye bread, quartered. Broil one minute or until lightly toasted.

Carolyn Pinkerton

Oyster and Bacon
Hors D'Oeuvres

Yield: 1 dozen

1 (3½ ounce) can　smoked oysters
1 (1 pound) package　bacon
1 (8 ounce) can　water chestnuts (optional)

Cut each strip of bacon in half. Cut each water chestnut in half. Wrap bacon half around 1 whole smoked oyster and, if desired, half a water chestnut. Skewer bacon, oyster and water chestnut with a toothpick. Bake under broiler until bacon is browned. Can be served hot or cold.

Virginia Glynn Barr

13

Fiesta Crab Mold

Serves: 10

Use a fish mold and garnish for an extra festive occasion.

½ (10½ ounce) can	cream of mushroom soup
1 (8 ounce) package	cream cheese
1 envelope	gelatin
⅛ cup	water
1 small	onion, chopped
½ cup	mayonnaise
dash	salt
½ cup	celery, chopped
1½ cups	crabmeat, shredded

Heat soup. Add cream cheese and stir. Dissolve gelatin in water and add to soup. Add onion, mayonnaise, salt, celery and crabmeat. Pour into greased one quart mold. Chill overnight or at least 5 hours before serving. Serve with crackers or rounds.

Marilyn Spey

Pizzaria Crab

Serves: 12

12 ounces	cream cheese
2 teaspoons	Worcestershire sauce
½	onion, grated
	garlic salt to taste
1 tablespoon	lemon juice
½-¾ bottle	chili sauce
1 (6½ ounce) can	crabmeat, minced and drained
	parsley

Mix cream cheese, Worcestershire sauce, onion, garlic salt and lemon juice and spread on a small meat platter or large plate. Cover cream cheese mixture with chili sauce and sprinkle with crabmeat and parsley. Cover with plastic wrap and refrigerate until serving. Serve with crackers or corn chips. May be frozen.

Rhonda Mead

Tarragon Crab

Serves: 8

1 pound	fresh crabmeat, cooked
¼ cup	tarragon vinegar
⅓ cup	mayonnaise
3 tablespoons	pimento, chopped
2 tablespoons	green onion, chopped
1 teaspoon	salt
½ teaspoon	pepper
1 tablespoon	capers, drained

Marinate crabmeat in vinegar at least 30 minutes in the refrigerator. Add remaining ingredients, mixing well. Serve on crackers.

Martha Kilpatrick

Hot Cheesy Crab

Serves: 6

1 (8 ounce) package	cream cheese
¼ cup	butter
1 (5 ounce) jar	Old English cheese spread
1 medium	onion, chopped
dash	Tabasco sauce
1 tablespoon	Worcestershire sauce
dash	red pepper
1 (6 ounce) package	frozen crabmeat, thawed and drained

Combine cream cheese, butter, cheese spread, onion, Tabasco, Worcestershire sauce and red pepper in top of double boiler until cheese is melted. Add crabmeat. Cook until warm. Serve with corn chips.

Add more Tabasco sauce and Worcestershire sauce for a "Spicy" Hot Cheesy Crab.

Carolyn Crotzer

Party Shrimp Marinade

2 cups	onions, sliced
8	bay leaves
1½ cups	white vinegar
2½ teaspoons	celery seed
1½ teaspoons	salt
1 teaspoon	Tabasco sauce
2½ pounds	shrimp, boiled and peeled

Mix all ingredients and pour over shrimp. Stir. Cover and refrigerate for at least 24 hours. Serve with party rye bread.

Betty Sahm

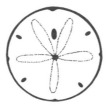

Poquito Shrimp Dip

Flavors blend when made in advance.

1 (8 ounce) package	cream cheese, softened
1 cup	shrimp, cooked and chopped
1 (8 ounce) carton	sour cream
¾ cup	green onion, chopped
¾ cup	celery, chopped
2 tablespoons	mayonnaise
1½ tablespoons	green pepper, chopped (optional)
3 tablespoons	parsley, chopped
2 teaspoons	horseradish
½ teaspoon	Tabasco sauce
	salt and pepper to taste

Combine all ingredients and stir. Serve with dip chips or rounds.

Christine Watson

Sea Spiced Dip

1 (8 ounce) package	cream cheese
½ cup	chili sauce
½ cup	mayonnaise
¼ cup	dried onion
2 tablespoons	horseradish
pinch	garlic salt
2 (4 ounce) cans	shrimp, drained and rinsed

In mixer, combine cream cheese, chili sauce and mayonnaise. Add onion, horseradish and garlic salt. Add shrimp and blend with mixer. Refrigerate overnight. Serve with chips.

Sandy Benton

Crabmeat Butter

Yield: 4 cups

This is truly worth the expense! Vary by adding 2-3 chopped green onions and a dash of cayenne pepper.

1 cup	butter, not margarine
4 (8 ounce) packages	cream cheese
2 pounds	lump crabmeat

In a double boiler, melt butter and cream cheese. Fold in the crabmeat. Serve in a chafing dish with rounds or chips.

Dee Dee Phillips

Shrimp Delight

Serves: 4

1 cup	mayonnaise
1 cup	Parmesan cheese
1	onion, chopped
	English muffins
	shrimp, cooked, peeled and deveined

Mix mayonnaise, cheese and onion. Toast muffins slightly. Place desired amount of shrimp on muffins and cover with mayonnaise mixture. Quarter muffins for appetizers or serve whole for a meal. Place on cookie sheet and broil until cheese is bubbly and begins to brown.

Sheila Gibson

Shrimp Marinade

1 (6 ounce) jar	Creole mustard
1 (5 ounce) jar	horseradish
1 cup	oil (add more if necessary)
1 teaspoon	Worcestershire sauce
½ cup	catsup
¼ cup	vinegar
1 medium	onion, thinly sliced
8-10 pounds	shrimp, boiled, peeled and salted generously

Combine all ingredients, adding shrimp last. Marinate at least 24 hours.

Faye Dawson

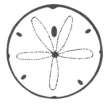

Shrimp Olé

1	onion, finely chopped
1	tomato, finely chopped
2-3 tablespoons	taco sauce
1 pound	shrimp, boiled, peeled and chopped
¼ teaspoon	garlic salt
3 (8 ounce) packages	cream cheese

Combine onion, tomato, taco sauce, shrimp and garlic salt over low heat. Add cream cheese and stir often. Cook until cheese melts.

Elizabeth Gonzales

Soy Shrimp

3 pounds	shrimp, peeled and butterflied
	oil
1 tablespoon	vinegar
1 cup	soy sauce
	juice of 2 lemons
1 tablespoon	onion, grated
	garlic powder to taste
	cayenne pepper to taste

Place shrimp in a cookie sheet or shallow pan. Fill pan about ¼ inch with oil. Combine vinegar, soy sauce, juice from lemons and onion and pour over shrimp. Season lightly with garlic powder and heavily with cayenne pepper. Broil for 5 minutes or sauté in saucepan.

John Fitzgerald

Pirate's Pantry Spread   *Serves: 12*

Keep these ingredients in the pantry for a last-minute appetizer.

1 cup	celery, chopped
1 medium	onion, chopped
1	green pepper, chopped
1 (6½ ounce) can	shrimp, drained and rinsed
1 (6½ ounce) can	crabmeat, drained and rinsed
1 cup	mayonnaise
1 tablespoon	Worcestershire sauce
1 cup	cracker crumbs

Combine all ingredients. Bake at 350 degrees F. for 20 minutes. Serve with crackers.

Linda Carr

Mary's Mushroom Pâté   *Yield: 2 cups*

4 slices	bacon, cooked and crumbled
½	onion, chopped
1 cup	fresh mushrooms, finely chopped
1 (8 ounce) package	cream cheese
½ cup	sour cream
dash	white pepper

Fry bacon and sauté onions and mushrooms in bacon drippings. Add cream cheese and stir until melted. Add sour cream and bacon and stir until blended. Place mixture in a 1½ quart baking dish and bake for 30 minutes or heat in microwave until hot. Serve with garlic or onion rounds.

Mary Grimsley

Ugly Dip   *Serves: 10*

Excellent, but UGLY!

4 large	tomatoes, peeled and finely chopped
4	green onions, minced
1 (4 ounce) can	jalapeños, drained and finely chopped
1 (4½ ounce) can	black olives, finely chopped
3 tablespoons	olive oil
1 teaspoon	garlic salt
2 teaspoons	vinegar
	salt and pepper

Mix all ingredients and chill overnight. Serve with tortilla chips.

Lou Baughman

Cheese Puffs
Yield: 2 dozen

1 (16 ounce) loaf	white bread, unsliced
8 tablespoons	butter
¼ cup	Mozzarella cheese
¼ cup	sharp Cheddar cheese
¼ cup	Swiss cheese
¼ cup	cream cheese
½ teaspoon	dry mustard
⅛ teaspoon	black pepper
	salt to taste
2	egg whites

Remove crust from bread and cut into 1 inch cubes. Combine butter and cheeses over moderate heat. Add the remaining ingredients. Beat egg whites and fold into mixture. Dip cubes into mixture to coat. Place on cookie sheet and freeze 15-20 minutes. Bake at 400 degrees F. for ten minutes or until golden brown.

Jo Fleet

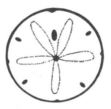

English Quarters
Yield: 2 dozen

6	English muffins
1 (4½ ounce) can	ripe olives, chopped
1 cup	Cheddar cheese, grated
¾ cup	mayonnaise
1 tablespoon	curry powder
½	onion, grated

Mix ingredients together and spread on muffins. Cut into quarters and freeze. When ready to prepare, bake at 350 degrees F. for 10 minutes.

Ruth Welsh

Salmon Log

1 (15½ ounce) can	red or pink salmon, drained and flaked
1 (8 ounce) package	cream cheese, softened
1 tablespoon	lemon juice
2 teaspoons	onion, minced
1 teaspoon	horseradish
¼ teaspoon	salt
¼-½ teaspoon	liquid smoke
½ cup	pecans or walnuts, chopped
3 tablespoons	parsley, chopped

Combine salmon and cream cheese, mixing well. Stir in remaining ingredients except nuts and parsley. Shape into a log and coat with nuts and parsley. Serve with crackers.

Paula Dorris

Poor Man's Caviar
Serves: 12

May be used as a first course garnished with wedges of hard-cooked egg and tomato.

¾ cup	ripe olives, sliced
¼ cup	capers, drained
1 (7 ounce) can	solid pack tuna, drained
1 (2 ounce) can	anchovy filets, undrained
1 large clove	garlic, crushed
½ teaspoon	dried thyme leaves
1 tablespoon	Dijon mustard
2 tablespoons	lemon juice
	pepper
3 tablespoons	fresh parsley, minced
3-4 tablespoons	mayonnaise
	hard cooked egg (optional)
	tomato (optional)

Combine olives, capers, anchovies and tuna. Chop until finely minced. Add remaining ingredients and mix thoroughly. Serve with crackers.

Charlene Chambless

Tuna Treasure

Yield: 3 cups

2 (8 ounce) packages	cream cheese
1 (6½ ounce) can	tuna, drained and flaked
1 medium	onion, chopped
1	tomato, chopped
2 tablespoons	hot peppers, chopped

Melt cream cheese in double boiler. Add remaining ingredients. Serve hot with chips.

Carol Daniel

Spinach Dip

Yield: 2 cups

1 cup	mayonnaise
1 cup	sour cream
1 (8 ounce) can	water chestnuts, chopped
1 (10 ounce) package	frozen chopped spinach, thawed and drained
1 (1⅝ ounce) box	dry vegetable soup mix

Mix all ingredients; chill and serve with crackers.

Becky Ratcliff

Chix Goodies

Yield: 3 dozen

4	chicken breasts, boned
1 cup	bread crumbs
½ cup	Parmesan cheese, grated
3 teaspoons	Accent
1¼ teaspoon	salt
1½ teaspoon	basil
½ teaspoon	thyme
½ cup	butter, melted

Cut chicken into bite-size pieces. Combine remaining ingredients except butter. Dip in melted butter, then crumb mixture. Place on a foil-lined cookie sheet; freeze and then bake at 350 degrees F. for 10 minutes or until golden brown.

Margie DeBolt

23

Hot Chicken Dip

Yield: 3½ cups

1 (10¾ ounce) can	cream of mushroom soup
1 (8 ounce) package	cream cheese
1 (5 ounce) can	chunk white chicken
1 (2¾ ounce) package	almonds, slivered
1 (2 ounce) can	sliced mushrooms, drained
½ teaspoon	Worcestershire sauce
1 tablespoon	sherry
⅛ teaspoon	garlic powder
⅛ teaspoon	white pepper

Combine all ingredients in a saucepan. Cook over medium heat, stirring often, until blended. Serve warm with chips.

Jean Blumer

Sesame Chicken Bites

Yield: 5 dozen

6	chicken breasts, boned
¼ cup	butter or margarine, melted
¼ cup	honey
1 teaspoon	teriyaki sauce
1 teaspoon	seasoned salt
½ teaspoon	garlic salt
¼ teaspoon	pepper
½ cup	sesame seeds

Cut chicken into bite-size pieces. Refrigerate overnight. Combine butter, honey and teriyaki sauce in a small pan; bring to a boil, stirring well. Remove from heat and set aside. Sprinkle chicken pieces with seasoned salt, garlic salt and pepper. Dip in honey mixture and coat with sesame seeds. Place chicken on a cookie sheet and bake at 350 degrees F. for 25 minutes, turning once. Reheat honey mixture and serve with chicken.

Elaine Doolin

"The Recipe"

This is an old family recipe.

1 can	beer
1 (6 ounce) can	pink lemonade
6 ounces	vodka

Combine beer and lemonade. Add vodka. Serve in champagne glasses.

Judy Trossbach

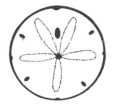

Pirate's Rum
Serves: 30

2 cups	butter
1 (16 ounce) box	confectioners sugar
1 (16 ounce) box	light brown sugar
2 teaspoons	ground cinnamon
2 teaspoons	ground nutmeg
2 teaspoons	ground cloves
1 quart	vanilla ice cream
	rum
	water

Combine all ingredients except rum and water in large pot over low heat until ice cream is melted and all ingredients are mixed well. To serve in individual mugs, fill mug with ¼ cup ice cream mixture, 1 jigger of rum and ½ cup hot water.

Carole Gordon

Pineapple Slush

Serves: 48

6 cups	sugar
2 cups	water, boiling
1 (12 ounce) can	frozen orange juice
4½ cups	water
½ cup	lemon juice
1 (8 ounce) jar	maraschino cherries, chopped
2 (46 ounce) cans	pineapple juice
2 (8¼ ounce) cans	crushed pineapple
8 (2 liter) bottles	ginger ale

In a large pot add sugar to 2 cups of boiling water. Stir until dissolved. Remove from heat. Add orange juice and water. Add lemon juice, cherries, pineapple juice and crushed pineapple. Freeze. Remove from freezer 2-4 hours before serving. Chip frozen mixture up into bowl and pour ginger ale over the chips before serving.

Beth Dodd

Piña Colada Punch

Serves: 20

1 (46 ounce) can	pineapple juice
1 (46 ounce) can	orange juice
2 (8 ounce) cans	banana daiquiri mix
2 (8 ounce) cans	cream of coconut
4 (8 ounce) cans	lime juice
2 cups	light rum

Place all ingredients in a large container. Place cupfuls of mixture into blender and blend until very smooth.

Vivian Lewis

Sweetheart Punch
Serves: 50

Float heart-shaped ice in punch bowl on Valentine's Day!

3 cups	sugar
1 quart	hot water
3 packages	unsweetened strawberry Kool-Aid
1 (46 ounce) can	pineapple juice
1 (6 ounce) can	frozen orange juice
3 (6 ounce) cans	water
2 cups	apricot nectar
1 quart	ginger ale

Dissolve sugar in hot water. Add Kool-Aid and refrigerate. Chill other ingredients and combine with sugar mixture before serving.

Brenda Lloyd

Jolly Ollie
Serves: 2

1 (6 ounce) can	frozen orange juice
1 cup	water
1 cup	milk
½ cup	sugar
½-1 teaspoon	vanilla
10-12	ice cubes

Combine above ingredients and blend until frothy.

Ellyn Smith

Deep Water Cooler
Serves: 1 or 10

1	orange slice
1	maraschino cherry
1 jigger	bourbon
	pink pineapple-grapefruit juice

Place orange slice and cherry in a tall glass filled with ice cubes. Add bourbon and fill with pineapple-grapefruit juice. Excellent as a summertime punch. For group, change ingredients to

2	oranges, thinly sliced
1 (8 ounce) jar	maraschino cherries and juice
1 ½ cups	bourbon
2 (46 ounce) cans	pink pineapple-grapefruit juice

Elaine Doolin

Brunch Punch
Serves: 6

1 ½ cups	milk
1 ½ cups	Half and Half
½ cup + 2 tablespoons	white creme de cacao
¼ cup + 2 tablespoons	bourbon
2 tablespoons	powdered sugar
2	egg whites
	cracked ice (optional)
	ground cinnamon or nutmeg (optional)

Combine first 6 ingredients in container of electric blender; blend until frothy. If desired, serve over cracked ice and sprinkle with cinnamon or nutmeg.

Martha Bayer

Camp Walton
Schoolhouse Punch

Serves: 20

A favorite served by the Junior Service League at the Camp Walton Schoolhouse Christmas Open House.

²/₃ cup	sugar
6 sticks	cinnamon
2 teaspoons	whole allspice
1-2 teaspoons	whole cloves
¼ teaspoon	salt
4 cups	cranberry juice
2½ cups	unsweetened pineapple juice
1 (12 ounce) can	frozen orange juice
5 (12 ounce) cans	water
1 (12 ounce) bottle	ginger ale

Combine spices, sugar, salt, cranberry juice and pineapple juice. Cover and simmer for 10 minutes. Remove whole spices and chill mixture. Dilute orange juice with water and freeze in a large ice ring. When ready to serve, pour fruit juice mixture into punchbowl, add chilled ginger ale and orange juice ice ring.

Betty Sahm

French 75's

3 bottles	champagne
1 bottle	vodka
1 bottle	brandy
4 cups	cold tea
1 bottle	club soda
5	lemons, sliced

Mix all ingredients and add a decorative molded ice ring. Add additional champagne, vodka, and brandy as punch melts down. This easy drinking punch packs a lethal wallop!

Jim Glynn

Margaritas Supreme
Serves: 4

Drink cautiously!

	lime wedges and slices
	salt
1 (6 ounce) can	frozen limeade concentrate, thawed
1 or 2 (6 ounce) cans	water, depending on taste
¾ cup	tequila
¼ cup	Triple Sec
	crushed ice

Rub rim of glass with lime wedge. Dip rim in salt poured in a saucer. Mix limeade, water, tequila and Triple Sec in a pitcher. Fill prepared glasses with crushed ice. Pour in margaritas and garnish with a slice of lime.

Champee Kemp

Sustainer
Champagne Punch
Serves: 20

2	cups sugar
3 bottles	sauterne
6 bottles	champagne
2 cups	brandy (chilled)
	Seven-Up or ginger ale

Mix sugar and sauterne; add brandy, ice and 3 bottles of champagne. Add ginger ale and 3 bottles of champagne before serving.

Mary Starnes King

Hot Cranberry Punch   *Serves: 20*

1 (32 ounce) bottle	cranberry juice
2¼ cups	pineapple juice
1 (6 ounce) can	sweetened lemonade
1 (32 ounce) bottle	ginger ale

Mix cranberry, pineapple and lemonade. Heat until very hot. Add ginger ale and serve.

Virginia Glynn Barr

Fish Head Punch   *Serves: 40*

This is always served at the Pinfish Invitational Tournament.

8 cups	orange juice
8 cups	pineapple juice, unsweetened
4 cups	pink grapefruit juice, unsweetened
6 cups	light rum
2 cups	dark rum
¾ cup	Grenadine syrup
	plastic fish, to taste

Combine all ingredients and serve in styrofoam treasure-chest-style cooler. Float toy fish for a special effect!

Rod Mitchell

Kahlua Slush

Serves: 4

1 cup	Kahlua or other coffee-flavored liqueur
1 pint	vanilla ice cream
1 cup	Half and Half
⅛ teaspoon	almond extract
dash	cinnamon
	ice cubes

Combine first 5 ingredients in electric blender. Add ice cubes slowly to bring mixture to the 6 cup level, blending all the time. Blend until smooth. Omit almond extract and use Amaretto for a different taste!

Martha Stivender

Juhl's Stand-Up Eggnog

Serves: 20-25

Serve with a spoon!

4 cups	whipping cream
12	eggs, separated
1½ cups	sugar
1 cup	bourbon (100 proof)

Beat whipping cream until stiff. In a separate bowl, using clean beaters, beat the egg whites until stiff. Add sugar from a sifter, a small amount at a time, until all sugar has been added. With clean beaters, beat the egg yolks until thick. Add bourbon very, very slowly, and continue to beat until all is added. Combine egg yolk mixture with whipped cream. Fold egg yolk and bourbon mixture into egg white and sugar mixture. Combine with a wooden spoon. Make early in the day and chill. Do not double. If mix separates, fold back together.

Jean Gordon

Soup & Sandwich

Soups

Sandwiches

Shrimp Gumbo
Serves: 6

A quick and easy version of gumbo!

½ cup	onion, chopped
2 tablespoons	butter or margarine
1 (16 ounce) can	tomatoes, sliced
1 (8 ounce) can	tomato sauce
1 (13¾ ounce) can	chicken broth
½ teaspoon	sugar
⅛ teaspoon	pepper
1	bay leaf
1 (15½ ounce) can	cut okra
1 (7½ ounce) can	shrimp or crab (fresh shrimp or crab may be used)
	cooked rice

Sauté onion in butter until tender in a 3 quart saucepan. Add tomatoes, tomato sauce, chicken broth, sugar, pepper and bay leaf. Bring to a boil. Reduce heat and simmer, uncovered, for 30 minutes. Remove bay leaf. Add okra and shrimp or crab; heat through. Serve gumbo over hot cooked rice in soup plates.

Betty Sahm

Oyster Bisque
Serves: 4

4 tablespoons	butter
½ cup	celery, chopped
1 tablespoon	parsley, chopped
½ teaspoon	Worcestershire sauce
¼ teaspoon	salt
dash	celery salt
dash	pepper
2 tablespoons	sherry
1 pint	oysters, drained
2 cups	half and half, warmed

Sauté celery and parsley in butter until soft. Stir in spices and sherry. Add oysters and cook until edges curl. Add milk. Do not boil.

Brenda Angel

Gazpacho   *Serves: 4*

*Best to prepare the soup a day in advance so the flavors can set.
Serve very cold and top with vegetables and croutons.*

3 large	tomatoes, peeled and chopped
1 large	cucumber, chopped
1 medium	onion, chopped
1 clove	garlic, chopped
1	green pepper, chopped
1 cup	tomato juice
1 teaspoon	parsley flakes
⅛ teaspoon	cayenne pepper
¼ teaspoon	salt
½ teaspoon	chives
2 tablespoons	white wine vinegar
¼ cup	olive oil
⅓ cup	cucumber, peeled and finely diced
⅓ cup	onion, finely chopped
⅓ cup	green pepper, finely chopped
⅓ cup	celery, finely chopped
1 cup	garlic croutons (optional)

Combine first five ingredients with tomato juice in a blender.
Blend well. Add spices, vinegar and olive oil. Blend. Chill. Serve in
ice cold mugs or bowls. Mix cucumbers, onion, green pepper and
celery together and sprinkle over each bowl of soup. Top with
croutons, if desired.

Tisha Fleet

General Babbitt's Cucumber Soup

Serves: 6

1 cup	chicken broth
¼ cup	onion, finely chopped
1 teaspoon	salt
½ teaspoon	dill weed, crushed
dash	garlic powder
1 teaspoon	fresh lemon peel, grated
2 tablespoons	lemon juice, freshly squeezed
1 cup	plain yogurt
1 cup	sour cream
2	cucumbers, peeled and chopped
	lemon slices
	cucumber slices

Combine chicken broth, onion, salt, dill weed, garlic powder, lemon peel and lemon juice in a blender. Blend until smooth. Combine yogurt and sour cream. Add to blender and turn on just long enough to blend. Add cucumber and quickly turn blender on and off just to combine. Cucumber will be finely grated but not liquified. Chill for 1 hour. Garnish with lemons and cucumbers.

Caroline Maney

Peaches and Cream

Serves: 6

3 cups	peach nectar
¾ cup	orange juice
pinch	cinnamon
six	peaches, peeled and pitted
½ cup	cream
½ cup	sour cream
1 (10 ounce) carton	frozen strawberries in syrup, defrosted

Combine peach nectar, orange juice and cinnamon in saucepan and bring to simmer. Cook peaches in juice for 5 minutes or until peaches are slightly softened. Puree peaches in blender and return to saucepan. Stir in remaining ingredients until blended. Pour soup into attractive glass bowl and refrigerate until serving time.

37

Emerald Coast Soup

Serves: 4

A cool, refreshing end to a long, hot summer day.

4 cups	chicken broth or stock
½ (1⅞ ounce) package	cream of leek soup mix
1 (10 ounce) package	frozen chopped broccoli
4-5 sprigs	parsley
dash	Worcestershire sauce
dash	pepper
½ cup	heavy cream
	sour cream (optional)

Combine broth, soup mix, broccoli and heat to boiling. Add parsley, Worcestershire sauce and pepper. Simmer until broccoli is tender. Blend until smooth. Add cream and chill if served cold. Reheat to serve warm. Garnish with a dollop of sour cream.

Martha Bayer

Clam Chowder

Serves: 4

1 small	onion, chopped
4 slices	bacon, coarsely chopped
2 (8 ounce) cans	minced clams, do not drain
4 medium	potatoes, finely diced
1½ teaspoons	salt
¼ teaspoon	pepper
2 tablespoons	cornstarch
3 cups	milk
2 tablespoons	butter or margarine
1 cup	Half and Half

Cook onion and bacon in a Dutch oven until bacon is lightly browned. Stir in clams, potatoes, salt and pepper; cover and simmer until the potatoes are tender. Dissolve cornstarch in a small amount of the milk. Add to clam mixture. Add butter and remaining milk and Half and Half. Cook over medium heat, stirring constantly, until thickened.

Mitzi Rowe

Barley Cheese Soup

Serves: 6

2 cups	broccoli, chopped
2 cups	hot water
1 (10¾ ounce) can	chicken broth
1 cup	carrots, sliced
½ cup	onion, chopped
½ cup	pearled barley
1 teaspoon	salt
1 small clove	garlic, minced
⅛ teaspoon	pepper
1½ cups	milk
⅓ cup	flour
1½ cups	Swiss cheese, diced

Combine broccoli, water, broth, carrots, onion, barley, salt, garlic and pepper in a 4 quart glass bowl or soup tureen. Cover with waxed paper and cook in a microwave at HIGH 18-20 minutes or until the barley is tender. Stir after 10 minutes of cooking. Combine ½ cup milk and flour, mixing until well blended; gradually add to soup with remaining 1 cup milk. Cover with waxed paper. Continue cooking on HIGH for about 5 minutes or until mixture is thickened. Stir 3 minutes, adding cheese. Cover; let stand 3-5 minutes before serving.

Marianne Dreyspring

Sausage Soup

Serves: 4

2 pounds	sausage, cooked and drained
3-4 large	potatoes, diced
2 (16 ounce) cans	red kidney beans
1 (16 ounce) can	tomatoes
1	green pepper, chopped
2	onions, chopped
4 cups	water
	salt, pepper and celery salt to taste
2	bay leaves
	pinch of thyme

Combine all ingredients in a 6 quart saucepan. Cover and cook over medium heat until tender or about 1 hour.

Jewel Howard

Pumpkin Soup
Serves: 6

Store this in the refrigerator for 3 days or the freezer for 3 months. Very appropriate at Halloween or Thanksgiving.

1 large	white onion, sliced
¾ cup	green onion, sliced, white part only
4 tablespoons	butter
1 (16 ounce) can	pumpkin
4 cups	chicken broth
1	bay leaf
½ teaspoon	sugar
¼-½ teaspoon	curry powder
⅛-¼ teaspoon	nutmeg
2 cups	milk, Half and Half or cream
	salt and ground pepper to taste
	sour cream, yogurt or whipped cream (optional)
	parsley sprigs (optional)

Sauté onions in butter until golden. Stir in pumpkin, broth, bay leaf, sugar, curry powder and nutmeg. Bring to a boil, reduce heat and simmer for 15 minutes, stirring occasionally. Place small amounts at a time into a blender and purée. Return to saucepan; add milk, salt and pepper. Simmer 5-10 minutes. Do not boil. Garnish with a dollop of sour cream, yogurt or whipped cream and a sprig of parsley.

Joy Banks

Pecan Soup   *Serves: 8*

2 cups	pecan halves
6 cups	beef broth
1 stick	butter
2 tablespoons	green onion, finely chopped
1 clove	garlic pressed
2 tablespoons	tomato paste
1 tablespoon	cornstarch dissolved in ¼ cup water
1	egg yolk
½ cup	half & half
½ teaspoon	salt
¼ teaspoon	white pepper
1 teaspoon	nutmeg

Grind pecans with broth in blender. Melt butter in large saucepan, add onions and cook 5 minutes over medium heat till soft. Add garlic and cook 1 minute. Slowly add nut/broth mixture, tomato paste, and cornstarch. Cook for 30 minutes, uncovered, on low heat. Beat egg yolk into cream and slowly whisk into soup; do not boil after this point. Season with salt, pepper and nutmeg. Serve hot or cold.

Caroline Maney

Special Potato Soup

Serves: 6-8

A hearty soup with a good flavor. Try adding cooked, chopped ham to vary the taste.

2	celery stalks, sliced
1 medium	onion, chopped
2 tablespoons	butter or margarine, melted
6 medium	potatoes, sliced
2	carrots, sliced
4 cups	water
5 cubes	chicken-flavored bouillon
¾ teaspoon	seasoned salt
½ teaspoon	dried thyme
½ teaspoon	rosemary, crushed
dash	garlic powder
2 cups	milk
1 cup	sharp Cheddar cheese, shredded

Sauté celery and onion in butter in a large Dutch oven until tender. Add next 8 ingredients; cover and simmer for 20 minutes or until vegetables are tender. Remove from heat and mash with a potato masher. Add milk and cheese; cook, stirring constantly, until cheese is melted.

Martha Bayer

Best Mushroom Soup

Serves: 8

1 large	onion, sliced into rings
½ cup	butter
2 tablespoons	flour
1 pound	fresh mushrooms, sliced
8 cups	beef stock
1 tablespoon	Worcestershire sauce
	salt and pepper to taste
½ cup	sherry

Sauté onions in ¼ cup butter. Blend in flour. Saute mushrooms in ¼ cup butter. Add mushrooms, beef stock, Worcestershire sauce, salt, pepper and sherry to onion mixture. Simmer 15 minutes.

Caroline Maney

Thanksgiving Gumbo

Serves: 6

1	turkey carcass
4 tablespoons	flour
4 tablespoons	oil
1 cup	green onion, chopped
1 cup	celery, chopped
4 tablespoons	parsley, chopped
3	bay leaves
½ teaspoon	thyme
1 tablespoon	gumbo filé
	salt and pepper to taste
1 pint	oysters (optional)
	cooked rice

Boil turkey carcass in enough water to cover for approximately 1 hour. Remove carcass and pick meat from bone. Set aside. Strain and reserve turkey broth. In a large skillet, make a roux by combining flour and oil and cooking over low heat, stirring constantly until mixture is a dark brown. Add onions, celery and parsley and sauté 5 minutes. Slowly add reserved broth; then add bay leaves, thyme, gumbo filé, salt and pepper and turkey. Cook over low heat for 1·1½ hours. Add oysters and cook 5 more minutes. Remove bay leaves and serve over hot rice.

Christine Watson

Beer Cheese Soup

Serves: 7 cups

⅔ cup	margarine
¼ cup	green onion with tops, chopped
⅔ cup	flour
1 (14½-ounce) can	chicken broth, ready made
1⅔ cup	evaporated milk, undiluted
1 (12 ounce) can	beer
1 (8 ounce) jar	processed cheese spread
1½ teaspoons	Worcestershire sauce
	broccoli flowerets, blanched

Melt margarine in large saucepan. Add onions. Cook until onions wilt, and remove from heat. Stir in flour. Gradually stir in chicken broth, milk, beer, cheese and Worcestershire sauce. Cook over medium heat, stirring constantly, until mixture reaches a boil. Serve with broccoli flowerets sprinkled over top.

Carol Ann DeBolt

Oyster Loaf

Serves: 4-6

1 large loaf	bread, unsliced
	melted butter
25-30	oysters
	salt and pepper
2	eggs, beaten
	cracker meal
	sliced dill pickles
	fish sauce (optional)
	lemon wedges (optional)
	stuffed olives (optional)
	parsley (optional)

Cut top off bread lengthwise, one inch thick. Set aside. Scoop center out of bread, leaving an oblong shell with one inch thick walls. Brush inside of bread with melted butter and bake at 400 degrees F. until brown. Wash, drain and dry oysters on paper towels. Sprinkle with salt and pepper, dip in egg and roll in cracker meal. Fry oysters in butter until light brown. Place hot oysters in bread shell, add sliced dill pickles and fish sauce, if desired. Replace bread top, garnish with stuffed olives, lemon wedges and parsley. Serve hot.

Monte Cristo Sandwich

Serves: 1

1	club sandwich, crust trimmed
3	eggs, beaten
2 tablespoons	milk
	oil
	sour cream
	powdered sugar
	strawberry jam

Press sandwich to make firm. Cut in half to make two rectangles. Beat eggs and milk together. Dip sandwich in egg mixture and then fry in ¼ inch of oil on all sides until golden brown. Top with sour cream that has been sweetened with powdered sugar and strawberry jam.

Tricia Twitty

44

BLT Soufflé
Serves: 2

Serve with a mug of soup and a jug of wine.

4 slices	bread
2	eggs
1½ cups	sharp Cheddar cheese, grated
1 teaspoon	mustard
dash	Worcestershire sauce
	salt and pepper to taste
4 slices	tomato
4 slices	onion
12 half-strips	bacon

Place bread on a greased cookie sheet. Combine eggs, cheese, mustard, Worcestershire sauce, salt and pepper in a bowl. Spread mixture onto each slice of bread. Place 2 slices of tomato on each slice of bread. Place onion slice on top of tomato. Crisscross 3 strips of bacon over each. Bake at 300 degrees F. for 30 minutes.

Patricia Dice

Blue Crab Sandwich
Serves: 4-6

2	egg whites, beaten until stiff
1 pound	crabmeat
½ cup	mayonnaise
	salt and pepper to taste
	toast
	paprika

Beat egg whites and combine with crabmeat, mayonnaise, salt and pepper. Pile on toast; sprinkle with paprika and broil for 3 minutes.

Patricia Twitty

Hot Brown Sandwich

Serves: 6

6 slices	bacon, halved
2 tablespoons	butter or margarine
2 tablespoons	flour
1/8 teaspoon	salt
dash	pepper
1/2 cup	turkey or chicken broth
1/2 cup	milk
1/3 cup	Parmesan cheese, grated
12-18 slices	turkey or chicken, cooked
6 slices	bread, toasted, crust removed
6 slices	tomato
	salt and pepper to taste
	paprika

Cook bacon in microwave. Set aside. Place butter in a 4 cup glass measure. Microwave at HIGH for 30-45 seconds or until butter is melted. Blend in flour, salt and pepper. Gradually stir in broth and milk. Microwave at HIGH for 3-4½ minutes, stirring at 1 minute intervals, until thickened. Stir in cheese; microwave at HIGH 1-2 minutes or until smooth. Stir well. Cover with plastic wrap. Set aside. Wrap turkey or chicken with plastic wrap and microwave to heat. Arrange turkey or chicken slices evenly on toast. Cover with cheese sauce, top with a tomato slice and sprinkle with salt and pepper. Place 2 pieces of bacon on each tomato slice and sprinkle with paprika.

Jean Blumer

Oriental Pocket

Serves: 4

2	whole large chicken breasts, boned
¼ cup	soy sauce
1 tablespoon	cornstarch
2 tablespoons	dry sherry
¼ teaspoon	crushed red pepper
1 teaspoon	sugar
¼ teaspoon	ginger
1 small head	green cabbage (1 pound)
4	green onions
2 medium	carrots
4 tablespoons	oil, divided
¼ teaspoon	salt
4	pitas
8 small	lettuce leaves

Slice chicken into ½ inch pieces. Set aside. Combine the next 6 ingredients and set aside. Thinly slice cabbage to make about 5 cups. Cut green onion into 3 inch crosswise strips. Slice carrots into matchstick-thin strips. Cook vegetables in 2 tablespoons oil in a 12 inch skillet over medium heat. Add salt and stir frequently and quickly until tender or about 5 minutes. Remove vegetables. In same skillet, add 2 tablespoons oil and cook chicken mixture, stirring quickly and often, until tender or about 3 minutes. Return vegetables to skillet and heat through. Preheat oven to 350 degrees F. Cut a pocket in each pita and warm in oven 5 minutes. To serve, place lettuce leaves in each pita and fill with chicken mixture.

Linda Carr

Gourmet
Chicken Sandwich

Serves: 6-8

6-8	chicken breasts, boned
½ cup	butter
1 cup	chicken broth
2-3 teaspoons	lemon juice
½ pound	fresh mushrooms, sliced
2 medium	onions, thinly sliced
½ cup	white wine
½ teaspoon	salt
¼ teaspoon	pepper
1 teaspoon	lemon pepper
1 teaspoon	parsley
½ teaspoon	garlic powder
½-1 teaspoon	gumbo filé
1	thick loaf French bread
	butter
	garlic powder
	Parmesan cheese, grated

In a medium skillet, brown chicken breasts in 1 tablespoon of butter. Remove and set aside. Add ¼ cup broth, lemon juice and remaining butter to the skillet. Stir until butter melts. Add mushrooms and onions, cover and cook over low heat until tender, stirring occasionally. Add wine and remaining broth; stir. Add salt, pepper, lemon pepper, parsley, garlic powder and gumbo filé. Stir well. Place chicken breasts in skillet and spoon sauce over each breast. Cover and simmer 30-45 minutes. Cut bread into one inch slices. Place on a cookie sheet, butter each slice and sprinkle lightly with garlic powder and Parmesan cheese. Place under broiler until golden brown. To serve sandwiches, place a slice of French bread on a plate, top with a chicken breast and pour sauce over the entire sandwich.

Debi Roberts

Salads

Salads

Avocados and Crabmeat With Herbed Mayonnaise Dressing
Serves: 4

½ pound	crabmeat
¼ cup	celery, finely chopped
¼ cup	mayonnaise
1 teaspoon	lemon juice
¼ teaspoon	salt
dash	pepper
2 large	avocados
2 cups	lettuce, shredded
2	eggs, hard boiled and sliced
1	lemon, cut into wedges
1	tomato, cut into wedges
4	black olives
	parsley

Combine crabmeat, celery, mayonnaise, lemon juice, salt and pepper. Pare, halve and seed avocados. Place ½ cup lettuce on each of 4 serving plates. Place avocado halves on top of the lettuce and fill with crabmeat mixture. Garnish with egg, lemon, tomato, olives and parsley. Serve with Herbed Mayonnaise Dressing.

Herbed Mayonnaise Dressing

1 cup	mayonnaise
⅛ teaspoon	tarragon
2 tablespoons	chives, chopped
⅛ teaspoon	chervil
2-3 tablespoons	tomato purée

Combine mayonnaise, tarragon, chives and chervil. Add enough tomato purée to make dressing pourable.

Donna Bridgford

Bastille Day Salad   *Serves: 8*

May be an entrée or salad! What a meal with a steak!

1 head	iceberg lettuce, cored and cubed
1 pound	lump crabmeat
35 small	shrimp, boiled and peeled
2	tomatoes, chopped
⅔ cup	red wine vinegar
⅔ cup	salad oil
½ cup	creole mustard
3	hard cooked eggs (optional)
8	anchovies (optional)

In a large bowl combine lettuce, crabmeat, shrimp and tomatoes. In a smaller bowl combine wine vinegar, oil and creole mustard; beat with a wire whisk. Pour oil and vinegar mixture over lettuce mixture. Chop eggs and anchovies and sprinkle over top of salad. Chill and serve.

Johnny Fitzgerald

Mushroom Zucchini Salad   *Serves: 6*

8 ounces	fresh mushrooms, sliced
1 medium	zucchini or cucumber, thinly sliced
1 medium	tomato, chopped
¼ cup	green onion, sliced
2 tablespoons	salad oil
2 tablespoons	vinegar
½ teaspoon	salt
½ teaspoon	pepper
½ teaspoon	marjoram, crushed

In salad bowl combine mushrooms, zucchini, tomato and green onion. Combine remaining ingredients in a jar and shake to mix well. Toss with vegetables, cover and chill for 4 hours.

Patio Salad

Serves: 6

1 (1 ounce) package	Italian dressing mix
6 tablespoons	salad oil
3 ounces	wine vinegar
½ cup	rosé or sauterne
	salt to taste
8 ounces	boiled shrimp
1 (6 ounce) can	pitted black olives, drained
1 (2 ounce) jar	sliced pimento
½ pound	fresh mushrooms, sliced
1 cup	lobster or crabmeat, cooked and flaked
1 (14 ounce) can	artichoke hearts, halved
	greens

Blend salad dressing mix, oil, vinegar, wine, and salt. Combine remaining ingredients and pour marinade over all. Chill 8 hours or more. Drain marinade. Spoon over lettuce cups or other salad greens.

Lou Baughman

Oriental Shrimp Salad

Serves: 4-6

1 (16 ounce) can	bean sprouts, drained and rinsed in cold water
2 cups	cooked shrimp, peeled and deveined
1 cup	chow mein noodles
1 (8 ounce) can	water chestnuts, drained and minced
¼ cup	green onions, minced with tops
¼ cup	celery, minced

Soy Mayonnaise Dressing

¾ cup	mayonnaise
1 tablespoon	lemon juice
1 tablespoon	soy sauce
¼ teaspoon	ground ginger

Combine salad ingredients. Mix all ingredients for dressing. Toss with salad.

Lou Baughman

53

Asparagus Mold

Serves: 8-10

3 (10 ounce) cans	cut asparagus, drained, reserve liquid
3 (1 ounce) packages	unflavored gelatin
3 tablespoons	water
1 cup	mayonnaise
¼ cup	lemon juice
½ cup	cream, whipped
	salt and pepper to taste
½ cup	slivered almonds

In a medium saucepan, add enough water to the asparagus liquid to make 2 cups and heat. Add the gelatin, which has been dissolved in 3 tablespoons of water; blend well. Remove from heat. Stir in mayonnaise, lemon juice, cream, salt and pepper. When partially set, fold in the asparagus and almonds. Pour into an oiled, 1½ quart mold and chill.

Liz Riley

Avocado Salad

Serves: 10

1 (3 ounce) package	lime gelatin
1 cup	hot water
2 cups	avocado, mashed
½ small	onion, grated
½ cup	mayonnaise
	juice of 1 lemon
½ teaspoon	salt
¾ cup	cream, whipped

Dissolve gelatin in hot water and cool until syrupy. Add avocado, onion, mayonnaise, lemon juice, and salt. Fold in whipped cream. Place in mold that has been oiled with small amount of mayonnaise. Refrigerate until firm.

Abigail Calhoun

Super Shrimp Salad

Serves: 4-6

1 pound	shrimp, cooked, peeled and deveined
3 cups	water
¼ pound	crabmeat
¼ cup	celery, chopped
½ cup	green pepper, chopped
2½ teaspoons	dill pickle, chopped
1	shallot, minced
1½ teaspoons	parsley, minced
½ cup	ripe olives, sliced
½ cup	stuffed olives, sliced
1 cup	Italian salad dressing
2 tablespoons	olive or corn oil
1½ teaspoons	lemon juice
	lettuce
	tomato wedges

Combine all ingredients except lettuce and tomato wedges. Place in an airtight container and refrigerate overnight. Line a serving platter with lettuce. Spoon salad over lettuce, top with tomato wedges.

Dolly Baker

Marty's Shrimp Salad

Serves: 6

1 cup	uncooked rice
1 pound	shrimp, boiled and peeled
1 (6½ ounce)	solid white tuna, drained and flaked
1 (3½ ounce) can	ripe olive, sliced
2 ribs	celery, diced
¾ cup	mayonnaise
⅓ cup	milk
2 tablespoons	virgin olive oil
2 tablespoons	lemon juice
2 tablespoons	Italian dressing
1½ teaspoons	curry powder

Cook and chill rice. Combine remaining ingredients and toss gently. Serve cold.

Carlaine Barber

Cranberry Mold
Serves: 12

Delicious with any poultry dish — especially nice during the holidays.

2 (3 ounce) packages	cherry gelatin
¾ cup	sugar
2 cups	hot water
½ cup	cold water
1-2 tablespoons	lemon juice
1 (20 ounce) can	crushed pineapple, drained, reserve syrup
1½ cups	raw cranberries, ground (measure and then grind)
1 small	orange, unpeeled, ground
½ cup	walnuts, coarsely chopped

Combine gelatin and sugar; dissolve in hot water. Add cold water, lemon juice and reserved pineapple syrup. Chill until partially set. Add pineapple and remaining ingredients. Turn into 2 quart mold. Chill overnight.

Martha Bayer

Citrus Shells
Serves: 4

Excellent with any seafood casserole.

2	grapefruit, halved
1 (3 ounce) package	lemon gelatin
1 (11 ounce) can	mandarin oranges, drained
	mayonnaise
	cherries

Scoop out grapefruit halves; reserve the fruit and shells. Very carefully clean pulp from grapefruit shells. Dissolve gelatin in boiling water, according to package directions. When slightly cool, add grapefruit sections and any juice from the grapefruit. Add oranges and fill grapefruit shells with the mixture. Chill. When congealed, cut each half into 2 wedges, top with a dollop of mayonnaise and a cherry.

Mary Bell Williams

Apricot Layered Salad

Serves: 8

3 (1 ounce) envelopes	unflavored gelatin
½ cup	water
1 (17 ounce) can	apricot halves, drained, reserve syrup
1 cup	sugar
	juice of 2 lemons
1 (3 ounce) package	cream cheese
1 cup	cream, whipped
	mint leaves

Soften gelatin in water and set aside. Combine apricot syrup and sugar, heat to boil and stir into gelatin. Set aside 2 apricot halves for garnish. Purée remaining apricots; stir in lemon juice and gelatin mixture except for 1 cup. Pour apricot mixture into a 9-inch square pan and chill until firm. Combine cream cheese and 1 cup reserved gelatin mixture. Beat until smooth. Fold in whipped cream. Pour over congealed apricot mixture. Chill until firm. Cut into squares to serve. Garnish with apricot slices and mint leaves.

Madelon David

Peach Salad

Serves: 4-6

1 (3 ounce) package	peach jell-o
1 (16 ounce) can	fruit cocktail
1 cup	buttermilk
1 (9 ounce) carton	whipped topping
1 cup	nuts, chopped

Mix jell-o and undrained fruit cocktail in a medium saucepan. Heat over medium heat to boiling, stirring constantly. Set aside to cool for 15-20 minutes. Mix buttermilk and whipped topping and fold into jell-o mixture. Add nuts. Refrigerate.

Mrs. Houston James

Driftwood Delight

Serves: 16

1 (3 ounce) package	lime gelatin
1 (3 ounce) package	lemon gelatin
2 cups	boiling water
1 (20 ounce) can	crushed pineapple, drained
1 (8 ounce) carton	small curd cottage cheese
1 cup	mayonnaise
1 cup	nuts, finely chopped
3 tablespoons	lemon juice
1 (14 ounce) can	condensed milk
2 tablespoons	horseradish
¼ teaspoon	salt

Dissolve the gelatin in hot water and let stand until cool. Add pineapple. Blend cheese with mayonnaise until smooth and add to gelatin mixture. Add all other ingredients and stir until mixture begins to congeal. Pour into molds and place in refrigerator overnight.

To vary, top with 1 cup sour cream mixed with 2 tablespoons horseradish.

Mary Grimsley

Double Decker Fiesta

Serves: 6-8

Serve this for a very festive luncheon!

FIRST LAYER

1 tablespoon	unflavored gelatin
¼ cup	cold water
1 cup	mayonnaise
½ cup	water
3 tablespoons	lemon juice
¾ teaspoon	salt
2 cups	chicken breast meat, boiled and diced
½ cup	celery, diced
1 tablespoon	onion, finely chopped

SECOND LAYER

1 envelope	unflavored gelatin
¼ cup	cold water
1 (16 ounce) can	whole berry cranberry sauce
1 (9 ounce) can	crushed pineapple in syrup
½ cup	pecans or walnuts, chopped
1 tablespoon	lemon juice

For first layer of salad, soften gelatin in cold water and dissolve over hot water. Blend in mayonnaise, water, lemon juice and salt. Add remaining ingredients. Chill until set in a 10 x 6 x 1 ½ inch or 8 x 8 inch dish. For the second layer, soften gelatin in cold water and dissolve over hot water. Add remaining ingredients and mix well. Cool and pour over first layer. Chill until firm. Layers may be reversed.

Dinah Remington

Lime-Cucumber Salad   *Serves: 10-12*

A cool, refreshing, summer salad!

1 (3 ounce) package	lime gelatin
¾ cup	hot water
2 (3 ounce) packages	cream cheese, softened
1 cup	mayonnaise
1 tablespoon	horseradish
½ teaspoon	salt
1 tablespoon	lemon juice
¾ cup	cucumber, grated
¼ cup	onion, minced
½ cup	parsley, chopped
½ cup	green pepper, chopped

Dissolve gelatin in hot water. Beat cream cheese until smooth and add to gelatin. Add mayonnaise, horseradish and salt. Beat until smooth. Blend in lemon juice. Chill until mixture resembles egg whites. Stir in vegetables. Pour into greased mold. Refrigerate overnight.

Betty Smith

Egg Ring   *Serves: 8-10*

10	hard cooked eggs, grated
½ cup	chili sauce
½ cup	mayonnaise
1 tablespoon	onion, grated
	salt to taste
	red pepper to taste
	pepper to taste
2 tablespoons	unflavored gelatin
⅓ cup	cold water
⅔ cup	chicken broth, warmed
	chicken, shrimp or crabmeat salad

Mix eggs, chili sauce, mayonnaise, onion and spices lightly in a bowl. Dissolve gelatin in water. Add chicken broth and stir until dissolved. Pour liquid over egg mixture, stir and pour into a greased ring mold. Refrigerate overnight. Fill center of ring with chicken, shrimp or crabmeat salad.

Mary Starnes King

Molded Gazpacho Salad   *Serves: 8-10*

1 ½ tablespoons	unflavored gelatin
¼ cup	cold water
1 ½ cups	tomato juice
1	cucumber, peeled and finely chopped
1 large	green pepper, finely chopped
2 tablespoons	green onions, finely chopped
½ cup	celery, finely chopped
dash	hot sauce
¼ cup	olive oil
1 ½ tablespoons	wine vinegar
1 tablespoon	fresh lemon juice
1 teaspoon	salt

Soften gelatin in cold water; set aside. Heat tomato juice in a large saucepan. Add gelatin and stir until dissolved. Add vegetables and seasonings. Mix well. Chill until slightly thickened; stir and pour into an oiled, 6 cup mold. Chill until firm. Unmold salad and serve with Creamy Dressing.

Creamy Dressing

½ cup	mayonnaise
¾ cup	sour cream
¾ cup	fresh parsley, minced

Mix together all ingredients.

Dinah Remington

Matt's Favorite Jell-o Salad

Serves: 12-15

2 (3 ounce) packages	orange gelatin
1 (20 ounce) can	crushed pineapple, drained, reserve syrup
1 cup	walnuts, chopped and divided
1 (8 ounce) package	whipped topping mix
1 (8 ounce) package	cream cheese, softened
1 tablespoon	lemon juice, freshly squeezed
¾ cup	sugar
2 tablespoons	flour
2	eggs, beaten

Prepare gelatin according to package directions; chill until mixture begins to congeal. Add pineapple to chilled gelatin; pour into oiled 13 x 9 x 2 pan. Sprinkle with ½ cup walnuts. Chill until mixture is completely congealed. Prepare whipped topping mix according to package directions; blend in cream cheese. Spread on gelatin. Cover and chill. Add enough water to reserved pineapple syrup to make 1 cup. Combine lemon juice, sugar, flour and eggs; add to pineapple syrup. Cook over low heat until thick. Chill thoroughly and spread over cream cheese mixture. Sprinkle with remaining walnuts.

Linda Carr

Sawdust Salad

1 (3 ounce) package	lemon gelatin
1 (3 ounce) package	orange gelatin
2 cups	hot water
¼ cup	cold water
1 (8¼ ounce) can	crushed pineapple, drained
3	bananas, sliced
1 (10 ounce) package	miniature marshmallows
2	eggs, well beaten
5 tablespoons	flour
1 cup	sugar
2 cups	pineapple juice
2 packages	whipped topping mix
1 cup	milk
1 (8 ounce) package	cream cheese
1 (3 ounce) package	cream cheese
	yellow cheese, grated, or coconut

Dissolve gelatin in water and add crushed pineapple. Place the bananas on top of the gelatin and pineapple. Top with marshmallows and let harden. Combine the eggs, flour, sugar and pineapple juice. Cook over medium heat until thick. Let cool. Spread on top of gelatin mixture. Combine whipped topping mix and milk. Add cream cheese and whip. Spread over all. Sprinkle with grated yellow cheese or coconut.

Beth Dodd

Piña Colada Salad

Serves: 6-8

Great for holiday entertaining!

1 envelope	unflavored gelatin
½ cup	cold water
1 (15½ ounce) can	unsweetened pineapple chunks, reserve syrup
½ cup	sugar
	juice of 1 lemon
2 (3 ounce) packages	cream cheese
1	orange, peeled, sectioned and chopped
½ cup	pecans, chopped
½ cup	coconut

Soften gelatin in water. Let stand 5 minutes. Add enough water to pineapple syrup to make 1 cup. Heat to boiling; add gelatin and stir. Remove from heat and stir in sugar, lemon juice and cream cheese. Blend. Chill until partially set. Add pineapple, oranges, pecans and coconut. Spoon into lightly greased 1 quart mold. Chill.

Dinah Remington

Fig Salad

A Different Salad

1 package	dried figs
1 bottle	white wine
1 package	cream cheese
1 (2½ ounce) container	black walnuts
1 head	Romaine lettuce

Soak dried figs in wine for approximately 20 minutes, then stuff figs with a mixture of the cream cheese and black walnuts. Place on a bed of Romaine lettuce.

These are tasty as a garnish without lettuce.

Linda Carr

Tuna Mousse

Serves: 8

Garnish with peeled, boiled shrimp and homemade mayonnaise to add elegance to this thrifty lunch.

½ envelope	unflavored gelatin
1 (3 ounce) package	lemon gelatin
¾ cup	water
1 tablespoon	cider vinegar
1 (10¾ ounce) can	cream of chicken soup
¾ cup	mayonnaise
½ cup	celery, chopped
1 tablespoon	onion, grated
½ cup	ripe olives, chopped
½ cup	slivered almonds
1 (6¼ ounce) can	tuna, rinsed and drained
dash	dill weed
dash	paprika
½ teaspoon	curry powder
	mayonnaise
	tomatoes, quartered
	(optional)

Mix unflavored gelatin with lemon gelatin. Add water and bring to boil. Add and mix remaining ingredients. Grease a 5 cup mold with mayonnaise. Pour in mixture and chill until firm. Turn onto platter and garnish with tomato quarters.

Patricia Twitty

Strawberry Pretzel Salad *Serves: 10-12*

2½ cups	pretzels, crushed
¾ cup	margarine
¼ cup	brown sugar
1 (6 ounce) package	strawberry gelatin
2 cups	boiling water
1 (10 ounce) carton	frozen strawberries
1 cup	sugar
1 (8 ounce) package	cream cheese, softened
1 (8 ounce) carton	frozen whipped topping, thawed

Combine pretzels, margarine and brown sugar. Mix well and pat into a buttered 9 x 13 x 2 inch baking dish. Bake at 350 degrees F. for 10 minutes. Let cool. Dissolve gelatin in water. While still warm, add frozen strawberries, stirring slightly to break up berries. Cool in refrigerator until mixture begins to set. Cream the sugar and cream cheese. Fold in whipped topping. Spread this mixture over the cooled crust making sure the crust is sealed well with the mixture. When gelatin mixture begins to set, pour over the cheese mixture. Chill until firm. Serve.

Substitute orange gelatin and mandarin oranges for a sunny pretzel salad!

Mitzi Rowe

Mandarin Orange Salad *Serves: 4-6*

1 (3-ounce) package	apricot jello
⅔ cup	boiling water
1 (11 ounce) can	mandarin oranges, drained
1 medium	banana, cut in chunks
1 (3 ounce) package	cream cheese

Mix together in blender just until blended. Pour in mold. Refrigerate.

Vicki Stevens

Broccoli Salad
Serves: 8

2 large bunches	raw broccoli, use only the tops
	juice of 1 lemon
4	green onions, finely chopped
1 pound	fresh mushrooms, sliced
	equal parts sour cream and mayonnaise, enough to coat the broccoli and mushrooms
½ teaspoon	salt
¼ teaspoon	pepper
2	tomatoes, chopped

Mix together all ingredients except tomato. Refrigerate for several hours or overnight. Just before serving, cover top of salad with chopped tomato. Sprinkle top with additional salt and pepper.

Marie Johnson

Elegant Artichoke Mushroom Salad
Serves: 6-8

1 quart	fresh mushrooms, sliced
1 pint	cherry tomatoes
2 (14 ounce) cans	artichoke hearts, drained and quartered
¼ cup	lemon juice
¼ cup	olive oil
¼ cup	red wine vinegar
1 clove	garlic, crushed
1 tablespoon	parsley
1 tablespoon	green onion, chopped
½ teaspoon	oregano
½ teaspoon	salt
¼ teaspoon	pepper

Place mushrooms, tomatoes and artichoke hearts in a salad bowl. Combine remaining ingredients in a blender and blend. Pour over vegetables. Refrigerate at least 4 hours before serving.

Lynne Amiel

Salad Niçoise

Serves: 8

2 pounds	new potatoes, sliced
2 cups	green beans
1 cup	artichoke hearts
1 large	onion, sliced
½ pound	mushrooms, sliced
	garlic dressing
	salad greens
1½ pounds	tuna or fresh crab
1 pint	cherry tomatoes
1 cup	ripe olives
6	hard cooked eggs, quartered
1	green pepper, sliced

Steam potatoes, beans and artichoke hearts until just crisp. Do not overcook. Marinate potatoes, beans, artichokes, onion and mushrooms in Garlic Dressing overnight. When ready to serve, drain vegetables and retain dressing. Toss together marinated vegetables and all other ingredients. Serve with dressing.

Garlic Dressing

1 tablespoon	dry mustard
1 teaspoon	sugar
1 tablespoon	salt
	pepper
2 cloves	garlic, minced
½ cup	tarragon vinegar
½ cup	lemon juice
2 cups	olive oil

Combine all ingredients and mix well.

Carole Gordon

The Best
Potato Salad
Serves: 10

1 tablespoon	parsley, chopped
2 cups	mayonnaise
¼ teaspoon	pepper
2 tablespoons	cider vinegar
1 envelope	Hidden Valley dressing mix
2 teaspoons	sugar
1 teaspoon	salt
2 teaspoons	prepared mustard
8 large	potatoes, boiled and chopped
4	eggs, hard cooked and chopped

Mix all ingredients except potatoes and eggs. Pour mixture over potatoes and eggs and toss. Serve immediately or chill.

Celery, green pepper and green onion may be added to this for a different taste.

Sharilyn Darnell

Sea Breeze Salad
Serves: 6-8

A delightful substitute when you are tired of potato salad!

2 (8½ ounce) cans	tiny English peas
1 cup	sour cream
1 cup	mayonnaise
1 teaspoon	Worcestershire sauce
3-4 dashes	Tabasco sauce
1 tablespoon	onion, minced
¼ cup	vegetable oil
4	hard cooked eggs, chopped
	lettuce

Heat peas until warm; drain and cool. Set aside. Combine sour cream, mayonnaise, Worcestershire sauce, Tabasco sauce, onion and oil. Stir until blended. Add peas and eggs and toss until blended. Refrigerate overnight and serve over lettuce.

Lynn Mayfield

Antipasto Salad

Serves: 10

1 (16 ounce) can	cut green beans, drained
1 (16 ounce) can	red kidney beans, drained
1 (7 ounce) can	pitted ripe olives, drained
1 (6-8) ounce can	mushrooms, drained
1 (4 ounce) jar	pimento, drained and diced
1 (15 ounce) can	artichoke hearts, drained and quartered
1½ cups	celery, sliced diagonally
1 medium	onion, thinly sliced
¼ cup	tarragon vinegar
1½ teaspoons	Accent
1 teaspoon	sugar
1 tablespoon	Fines Herbes
¼ teaspoon	Tabasco sauce
½ cup	salad oil
¼ cup	parsley, chopped
2 tablespoons	capers

Combine vegetables. Mix vinegar, Accent, sugar and Fines Herbes in a jar; shake well. Add Tabasco sauce and oil and shake until blended. Pour over vegetables and refrigerate several hours. Add parsley and capers just before serving.

Ginny Mitchell

Summertime Tomatoes

Serves: 3-4

3 medium	tomatoes, sliced
2 tablespoons	tarragon vinegar
3 tablespoons	olive oil
½ teaspoon	salt
¼ teaspoon	dried tarragon
1 tablespoon	parsley, minced
1 tablespoon	green onion, minced
	pepper, freshly ground to taste

Arrange tomatoes in a serving dish. Mix remaining ingredients and pour over tomatoes. Let stand at room temperature at least 1 hour before serving.

Elaine Doolin

Greek Salad
Serves: 6-8

1 head	lettuce, broken into pieces
½	cucumber, sliced
2	tomatoes, chopped
1	green pepper, cut in rings
4	green onions, sliced with tops, or 1 onion, sliced in rings
½-¾ cup	Feta cheese, broken in small chunks
½ cup	ripe Greek olives, whole oregano

Dressing

½ cup	olive oil
4 tablespoons	vinegar

Mix all salad ingredients except oregano. Mix dressing ingredients and pour over salad. Sprinkle with oregano.

Marlene Barron

Wilted Lettuce Salad
Serves: 4

3 slices	bacon
3 tablespoons	bacon drippings
¼ cup	cider vinegar
	salt to taste
½ teaspoon	pepper
1 teaspoon	brown sugar
4 cups	lettuce, torn into pieces

Cook bacon until crisp and drain. Combine bacon drippings, vinegar, salt, pepper and sugar in a small pan and bring to a boil. Pour over torn lettuce and toss. Garnish with crumbled bacon. Serve immediately.

This is also wonderful if spinach is used instead of lettuce!

M.E. Douglas

Florida Toss Salad

Serves: 6

1 head	Romaine lettuce, torn into pieces
1 head	leaf lettuce, torn into pieces
1 (11 ounce) can	mandarin oranges, drained
⅓ cup	slivered almonds
1 cup	fresh mushrooms, sliced
1 large	avocado, diced (optional)
4	green onions, chopped
¾ cup	Romano cheese, grated

Dressing

¼ cup	vegetable oil
2 tablespoons	sugar
2 tablespoons	vinegar
½ teaspoon	salt

Toss all salad ingredients. Mix dressing ingredients and pour over salad.

Ellyn Smith

Rice and Artichoke Salad

Serves: 8

1 (8 ounce) box	chicken-flavored rice mix
1 (6 ounce) jar	marinated artichoke hearts, reserve liquid
2½ cups	mayonnaise
1 (14 ounce) can	artichoke hearts
2 (4½ ounce) cans	ripe olives, chopped
½	green pepper, chopped
1 bunch	green onions, chopped

Cook rice according to package directions. Set aside. Blend marinated artichoke liquid into mayonnaise. Combine rice, mayonnaise mixture, artichoke hearts, olives, green pepper and green onions. Chill. Flavor is best if prepared ahead and chilled overnight.

This recipe can be varied by adding chicken or shrimp.

Barbara Ridge

Sunny Spinach Salad   *Serves: 8-10*

	spinach
	lettuce
	fresh mushrooms, sliced
	mandarin orange sections
	bacon, cooked and crumbled
1 cup	mayonnaise
½ cup	sugar
½ cup	milk
4 tablespoons	vinegar
1	onion, chopped
	salt to taste
	Parmesan cheese, grated

Toss spinach, lettuce, mushrooms, oranges and bacon. Set aside. Combine mayonnaise and sugar; slowly add milk and vinegar. Mix well. Add onion and salt. Chill. When ready to serve, toss spinach mixture with dressing and top with Parmesan cheese. Vary amounts of ingredients to suit taste.

Nancy Jones

Chicken Chutney Salad   *Serves: 4*

2 cups	chicken breast meat, cooked and diced
1 (8 ounce) can	pineapple tidbits, drained
1 cup	celery, sliced
½ cup	green onion, sliced
½ cup	salted peanuts
⅔ cup	mayonnaise
2 tablespoons	chutney, chopped
½ teaspoon	lime rind, grated
½ teaspoon	curry powder
¼ teaspoon	salt
	black pepper to taste
	garlic salt to taste
	lettuce greens

Toss all ingredients except greens. Chill and serve on greens.

Linda Scoville

French Beef Salad

Serves: 8-10

Must prepare ahead:

2 pounds	small boiling potatoes, sliced ¼ inch thick
2 pounds	sirloin
1 pound	green beans, cleaned and snapped
1 cube	beef bouillon cube
¼ cup	boiling water
1 teaspoon	garlic, minced
4 tablespoons	shallots, minced
2 tablespoons	Dijon mustard
2 teaspoons	salt
1 teaspoon	black pepper
⅓ cup	red wine vinegar
1 cup	olive oil
1 large	red onion, thinly sliced
1 pint	cherry tomatoes
1 (8 ounce) package	mushrooms, sliced

Boil potatoes until tender; drain and place in a large bowl. Meanwhile, boil sirloin until rare. Cook green beans until tender, about 7 minutes; plunge into ice water. Drain. Dissolve bouillon cube in boiling water. Combine garlic, shallots, beef bouillon, mustard, salt, pepper, vinegar and olive oil to make a vinaigrette. Pour vinaigrette over potatoes and toss. Slice sirloin into ½-inch cubes. Add sirloin, green beans, onions, tomatoes and mushrooms to bowl. Toss gently, but thoroughly. Allow to marinate in refrigerate 1 to 3 days. Remove from refrigerator and bring to room temperature before serving.

Carlaine Barber

Korean Salad

Serves: 4

	fresh spinach, washed and torn into bite-size pieces
1 (16 ounce) can	bean sprouts or fresh bean sprouts
½ pound	bacon, fried and crumbled
1 (8 ounce) can	water chestnuts, drained and sliced
2	eggs, hard cooked and sliced
1	green onion, chopped
	fresh mushrooms (optional)
	avocado (optional)

Dressing

1 cup	salad oil
⅓ cup	catsup
¼ cup	vinegar
⅔ cup	sugar
1 tablespoon	Worcestershire sauce
1	green onion, chopped

Combine all ingredients for salad. Mix all ingredients for dressing in a blender. Pour over spinach mixture and mix thoroughly.

Lee Bruner

Taco Salad

Serves: 8-10

1	onion, chopped
4	tomatoes, chopped
1 head	lettuce, broken into pieces
4 ounces	Cheddar cheese, grated
	crushed corn chips to taste
1 large	avocado, sliced
1 pound	ground beef
1 (15 ounce) can	kidney beans or pinto beans
¼ teaspoon	salt
Dressing #1: 1 cup	mayonnaise
⅓ cup	catsup
1 tablespoon	onion, grated
2	eggs hard cooked and chopped
Dressing #2: ½ cup	taco sauce (mild or hot)
½ cup	salad dressing

Combine first 4 ingredients, adding corn chips and avocado. Brown ground beef, add beans, salt, and simmer 10 minutes. Combine with cold salad and toss with either dressing.

Bobbi Nelson

Mexican Toss

Serves: 6

½ medium head	lettuce torn into small pieces
2	tomatoes, cut in small sections
¼ cup	green onion, chopped
½ cup	Cheddar cheese, shredded
1 (6½ ounce) can	white tuna
½ cup	pitted black olives, sliced
1 cup	corn chips, crushed
Avocado Dressing: ½ cup	avocado, mashed
1 teaspoon	lemon juice
½ cup	sour cream
1 clove	garlic, crushed
1 teaspoon	sugar
½ teaspoon	chili powder
¼ teaspoon	salt
¼ teaspoon	Tabasco sauce

Prepare salad. Combine dressing ingredients, and beat with electric mixer. Toss salad and dressing, garnishing with extra olives and cheese.

Dinah Remington

Kelsey's Salad Dressing

1½ cups	mayonnaise
2 teaspoons	prepared mustard
5 tablespoons	honey
2 tablespoons	parsley
¼ cup	buttermilk
1 teaspoon	lemon juice

Combine all ingredients and chill. Serve with mixed salad greens or with cole slaw.

Debby Barrineau

Custard Fruit
Salad Dressing   Yield: 1½ cups

Delicious with melon balls and fresh summer fruit.

¼ cup	pear juice
¼ cup	orange juice
2 tablespoons	lemon juice
¼ teaspoon	hot, dry mustard
¼ teaspoon	salt
2	eggs
½ cup	sugar
½ cup	mayonnaise

Blend all but mayonnaise. Cook in double boiler over medium heat until thickened. Chill. Before serving, fold in mayonnaise.

Margie Zant

77

Lemon-Dijon Dressing   *Yield: 1 cup*

1	egg
2 teaspoons	Parmesan cheese, grated
½ teaspoon	salt
¼ teaspoon	pepper
2 tablespoons	Dijon mustard
3 tablespoons	lemon juice
1 teaspoon	Worcestershire sauce
1 teaspoon	sugar
½ cup	vegetable oil

Combine all ingredients and beat vigorously with a wire whisk until completely blended. Place in a covered jar and chill at least 2 hours. Shake vigorously just before serving. Serve over fresh greens.

Mary Grimsley

Honey Blue Cheese   *Yield: 1 ½ cups*

½ cup	prepared French dressing
¾ teaspoon	dill seed
¾ teaspoon	celery seed
⅜ teaspoon	granulated garlic
⅛ teaspoon	salt
⅛ teaspoon	pepper
⅛ teaspoon	dried onion flakes
1 tablespoon	honey
½ cup	blue cheese, crumbled
1 tablespoon	red wine
1 tablespoon	red wine vinegar

Combine ingredients and chill. Serve over mixed greens. Garnish with pecans or walnuts.

Wynn Noland · Finnegan's

Breads

Breads

Cinnamon Bread
Yield: 2 loaves

2¼ cups	milk
⅓ cup	sugar
¼ cup	shortening
2 teaspoons	salt
1 package	yeast
5¾-6½ cups	flour

Filling

½ cup	sugar
3 teaspoons	cinnamon

Combine milk, sugar, shortening and salt in a small pan. Heat to warm (120 degrees F.). Add yeast and let stand for 15 minutes. Add 2½ cups flour. Beat at low speed with electric mixer for ½ minute, scraping sides of bowl constantly. Beat 3 minutes at high speed. By hand stir in enough of the remaining flour to make a moderately stiff dough. Turn to a lightly floured surface; knead until smooth and elastic, approximately 10 minutes. Shape into a ball; place in a greased, pre-warmed bowl, turning once to grease top. Let rise until doubled in size, approximately 1¼ hours. Divide the dough in half. Roll each half in a 15 x 7 inch rectangle. Combine ingredients for filling and spread half of the mixture over each rectangle. Roll into loaves, sealing edges. Place in greased loaf pans. Let rise until double, about 45 minutes. Bake at 375 degrees F. for 30 minutes or until loaf sounds hollow when tapped.

René Westerfeld

Braided
Egg Butter Bread

Yield: 2 loaves

2 packages	yeast
½ cup	warm (110-115 degree F.) water
1½ cups	milk
½ cup	butter or margarine
½ cup	sugar or honey
3 large	eggs, slightly beaten
1 tablespoon	salt
7-8 cups	unbleached white flour
1 tablespoon	butter, melted
1	egg yolk
2 teaspoons	water
	poppy or sesame seeds

Dissolve yeast in water and let sit about 15 minutes. Warm milk, butter and sugar to 120-130 degrees F. Let cool slightly. Add eggs, salt, yeast mixture and 2 cups flour and mix. Add remainder of flour slowly and knead for 10 minutes. Turn dough in a greased bowl and let rise covered in a warm place for 1½ hours or until doubled in size. Punch down dough. Cover and let rise 10 minutes. Form in 3 large or 4 small loaves.

To make braided loaves, divide dough into 3 or 4 balls and divide each ball into 3 pieces. Roll each piece into 15-inch rope. Lay the first 2 ropes into an X shape. Lay the third rope parallel to the first rope and over the second. Continue to braid. Brush loaves with 1 tablespoon of butter and let rise 30 minutes or until an indentation from the fingertips is left in the dough. Brush loaves with the egg yolk and water mixture. Sprinkle with seeds. Bake at 325 degrees F. for 25-30 minutes until browned.

Ann Roper

Honey
Whole Wheat Bread

Yield: 2 loaves

3 cups	unbleached white flour
3 cups	whole wheat flour
2 packages	yeast
1 tablespoon	salt
1 cup	milk
1 cup	water
½ cup	honey
3 tablespoons	margarine

Mix 1 ½ cups whole wheat flour and 1 ½ cups unbleached white flour in a large mixing bowl. Add yeast and salt. In a small saucepan, heat milk, water, honey and margarine on low heat until very warm (120-130 degrees F.). Slowly pour liquid into dry ingredients and mix with an electric mixer until well blended. Continue to mix on medium-high speed until dough is smooth and elastic, approximately 7 minutes. If mixing by hand, stir in remaining ingredients after first mixing and knead until smooth and elastic. Put dough in a greased bowl and turn to grease top. Cover and let rise in a warm place until double in size, approximately 1 hour. Punch down dough. Remove from mixing bowl and divide dough in half. Flatten dough with a rolling pin to a 9 x 13 inch rectangle to remove air bubbles. Roll tightly and shape into 2 loaves. Place loaves into 2 greased 8½ x 4½ inch loaf pans. Let bread rise covered in a warm place for 1 hour or until doubled in size. Bake at 350 degrees F. for 35 minutes. Remove bread from pans and cool on wire racks.

Suzanne Seemann

Cottage Cheese Dill Bread

Yield: 1 loaf

1 package	yeast
¼ cup	water
2 tablespoons	sugar
2 tablespoons	onion, chopped
2 teaspoons	dill seed
½ teaspoon	salt
¼ teaspoon	baking soda
1 cup	creamed cottage cheese, lukewarm
1 tablespoon	butter, softened
1	egg
2½-3 cups	flour
1 tablespoon	butter, melted

Dissolve yeast in warm (105-110 degrees F.) water. Combine remaining ingredients except flour and melted butter. Beat in enough flour to make a stiff dough. Cover and let rise until double, approximately 1 hour. Punch down and turn into well-greased 2-quart casserole. Brush with melted butter. Let rise until light, approximately 40 minutes. Bake at 350 degrees F. for 35-40 minutes.

Myra Arnold

Savory Herb Bread
Yield: 2 loaves

3 cups	warm (105-115 degree) water
2 tablespoons + 1 teaspoon	sugar
½ teaspoon	salt
2 packages	yeast
¼ teaspoon	ginger
6½-7 cups	flour
3 teaspoons	powdered chicken stock
1 teaspoon	thyme
1 teaspoon	parsley
1 teaspoon	rosemary
½ teaspoon	ground savory
½ cup	butter or margarine, softened
1	egg yolk, beaten
1 teaspoon	water

In a small bowl combine ½ cup lukewarm water, 1 teaspoon sugar, ½ teaspoon salt, ¼ teaspoon powdered ginger and 2 packages yeast. Let stand in a warm place until mixture bubbles. In a large bowl stir together 2 cups lukewarm water, 2 tablespoons sugar, 3 cups flour and 3 teaspoons powdered chicken stock, dissolved in ½ cup warm water. Mix thoroughly. Add yeast mixture and beat well. Add thyme, parsley, rosemary, savory, butter and 3½-4 cups flour. Stir until the dough comes away from sides of bowl. Knead dough about 8-10 minutes, using more flour if necessary to make the dough smooth and elastic. Place dough in a greased, covered bowl. Turn so the dough will be greased on top. Cover and let rise in a warm place about 1 hour or until doubled in bulk. Punch down and turn dough onto a lightly floured board. Knead several times. Divide in half and shape each half into a loaf. Place each into a well-greased loaf pan and brush with melted butter. Let rise covered until doubled in bulk, approximately 1 hour. Bake at 350 degrees F. for 50 minutes or until tops are brown and have a hollow ring when tapped. For a glazed crust, brush tops of loaves with mixture of 1 beaten egg yolk and 1 teaspoon water, 5 minutes before end of baking period.

Bill Allen

Black Russian Rye Bread

Yield: 2 loaves

2½ cups	unbleached flour
2 cups	whole bran cereal
2 packages	yeast
1 tablespoon	sugar
1 tablespoon	salt
1 tablespoon	instant coffee powder
2 teaspoons	onion powder
1 teaspoon	crushed fennel seed
2½ cups	water
1 cup	molasses
¼ cup	cooking oil
1 square	unsweetened chocolate
4 cups	rye flour
1	egg white
1 tablespoon	water

Lightly spoon 1 cup unbleached flour into measuring cup and level off. Combine with next 7 dry ingredients in a large mixing bowl. Heat in a saucepan over a low heat until very warm (120-130 degrees F.) water, molasses, oil and chocolate. Add warm liquid to flour mixture. Blend at low speed until moistened. Beat 3 minutes at medium speed. By hand stir in 4 cups rye flour. Knead on floured surface adding ½ to 1½ cups of the remaining un-bleached flour until dough is smooth and pliable, approximately 5 minutes. Place dough in greased bowl. Cover and let rise in a warm place until almost doubled, approximately 45 minutes. Punch down dough. Divide in half and shape each into a ball. Place balls in a greased 9-inch round cake pan. Cover. Let rise in warm place until almost doubled, approximately 30 minutes. Brush loaves with a mixture of 1 egg white and 1 tablespoon water. Bake at 375 degrees F. for 50-60 minutes, or until loaves sound hollow when lightly tapped. Remove from pans and cool.

Myra Arnold

Onion Rye Bread
Yield: 2 loaves

1½ cups	milk
3 tablespoons	butter or margarine
1½ cups	rye flour
3 cups	flour
1 package	dry yeast
3 tablespoons	sugar
1 teaspoon	salt
1 tablespoon	caraway seed
½ cup	onion, minced
	corn meal
	egg white, slightly beaten
1 tablespoon	water

Heat milk and butter until warm (120 degrees F.). In a large mixing bowl combine rye flour, 1 cup flour, yeast, sugar, salt, caraway seed, onion and warm milk. Mix on medium speed for 3 minutes. Gradually add remaining flour to form a stiff dough. Knead until smooth and elastic, about 5 minutes. Place dough in a greased bowl, turning once to grease top. Cover and let rise in a warm place until doubled, approximately 1½ hours. Punch down and roll into a 15 x 10 inch rectangle on a lightly floured board. Roll tightly, jellyroll style, beginning with long side. Seal edges and ends well. Place diagonally, seam-side down, on greased baking sheet sprinkled with corn meal. Cover and let rise in a warm place approximately 1½ hours or until doubled. Slash top diagonally before baking. Brush top with egg white and water mixture. Bake at 350 degrees F. for 30-35 minutes. Cool on a wire rack.

Suzanne Seemann

Monkey Bread
Serves: 6

1 cup	milk
1 cup	butter, divided and melted
1 teaspoon	salt
4 tablespoons	sugar
1 package	yeast
3½ cups	flour

Combine milk, ½ cup butter, sugar and salt in a saucepan. Heat until butter is melted. Stir in yeast and dissolve. Place flour in a large bowl; make a well in flour and pour in liquid. Stir until blended. Cover and let rise until doubled in bulk, approximately 1½ hours. Turn dough onto a floured surface and roll ¼ inch thick. Cut into 3-inch squares. Dip each square in remaining butter. Layer squares in a 10-inch tube or Bundt pan. Let rise until doubled in bulk, approximately 40 minutes. Bake at 375 degrees F. for 30-40 minutes.

Margaret Peel

Sadie's Yummy Rolls
Yield: 3 dozen

1 cup	warm water
1 package	yeast
1 teaspoon	salt
1 teaspoon	sugar
½ cup	shortening, melted
½ cup	sugar
2 cups	warm water
6½-7 cups	flour
	melted butter

Mix together 1 cup warm water, yeast, salt and 1 teaspoon sugar. Let set for 20 minutes. In a large bowl combine melted shortening, ½ cup sugar and 2 cups warm water. Combine this with yeast mixture and add flour. Mix until well blended. Refrigerate dough overnight or at least 4 hours. When ready to bake, pinch off about 1½ tablespoons of dough for each roll; place in muffin tins. Let rise for 2 hours. Brush with melted butter. Bake at 400 degrees F. for 15-20 minutes.

Sadie Carey

Ice Box Rolls

1 package	yeast
½ cup	water
1 cup	milk
⅔ cup	shortening
½ cup	sugar
1 teaspoon	salt
1 cup	mashed potatoes
6½ cups	flour
2 eggs	eggs

Dissolve yeast in water that has been heated to lukewarm (105 degrees F.). Scald the milk and add shortening, sugar, salt and potatoes. When the mixture has cooled to lukewarm, add dissolved yeast; mix and add enough flour to make a thin batter. Cover and let rise until double in bulk. Add the beaten eggs and stir in enough flour to make a stiff batter. Turn out on floured board and knead thoroughly until blisters appear on the surface. Put into a greased bowl large enough to allow for rising. Cover and set in refrigerator, or make rolls and let rise until double, approximately 2 hours. Shape rolls and place on a greased cookie sheet. Bake at 425 degrees F. for 15 to 20 minutes.

Faye Dawson

Jarrett House Biscuits   *Yield: 1½ dozen*

2 cups	self-rising flour
5 tablespoons	lard
½ cup	buttermilk
½ cup	sweet milk

Preheat oven to 450 degrees F. Cut the lard into the flour. Moisten with buttermilk-sweet milk combination. Mix together. Roll to ½ inch thickness on floured board. Cut with biscuit cutter. Bake on ungreased cookie sheet 12-15 minutes.

Nancy Matherne

English Muffin Loaves

Yield: 2 loaves

6 cups	flour
2 packages	dry yeast
1 tablespoon	sugar
2 teaspoons	salt
¼ teaspoon	baking soda
2 cups	milk
½ cup	water
	cornmeal

Combine 3 cups flour, yeast, sugar, salt and soda. Heat liquids until very warm (120-130 degrees F.). Add to dry mixture; beat well. Stir in remaining flour to make a stiff batter. Spoon into two 8¼ x 4½ inch loaf pans that have been greased and sprinkled with cornmeal. Sprinkle tops with cornmeal. Cover. Let rise in a warm place for 45 minutes. Bake at 400 degrees F. for 25 minutes. Remove from pans immediately and cool. Slice and toast.

Judy Muller

Mexican Corn Bread

Serves: 8

1 cup	corn meal
1 teaspoon	salt
1 teaspoon	baking soda
1 cup	creamed corn
2	eggs, beaten
½ cup	oil
¼ cup	flour
¾ cup	milk
¾ cup	Cheddar cheese, grated
2	jalapeño peppers, seeded and chopped
¼ cup	oil

Measure and combine ingredients. Pour ¼ cup oil into a 9 inch skillet and heat. Pour batter into the skillet and bake at 425 degrees F. for 30 minutes.

Sandy Benton

Gourmet French Bread

1	thin loaf French bread, sliced lengthwise
	margarine
1 cup	mayonnaise
½ cup	green onions, finely chopped
½ cup	Monterey Jack cheese, grated
½ teaspoon	Worcestershire sauce
	paprika
	Parmesan cheese

Spread margarine on both lengths of bread. Mix mayonnaise, onions, cheese and Worcestershire sauce. Spread mixture on bread. Sprinkle with paprika and Parmesan cheese and bake at 350 degrees F. for 15-20 minutes.

Nancy Matherne

Hush Puppies

2 (8½ ounce) boxes	instant corn muffin mix
2 (6 ounce) boxes	packaged pancake mix
1-2 cups	onion, chopped
2	green peppers, chopped
	buttermilk

Mix dry ingredients together. Add onion and pepper. Add enough buttermilk to make a stiff batter. Drop by spoonfuls into hot grease and cook until golden brown.

Bert McCall

Banana Nut Pancakes
Serves: 4

1 cup	flour
2 tablespoons	sugar
2 teaspoons	baking powder
½ teaspoon	salt
1 cup	milk
1	egg
2 tablespoons	oil
1	banana, mashed
¼ cup	nuts, chopped

Combine flour, sugar, baking powder and salt; set aside. In a large bowl stir egg, milk and oil until well blended. Add flour mixture and blend well. Stir in banana and nuts. Drop by scant ¼ cupfuls onto a hot, lightly greased griddle. Cook, turning once, until golden. Serve with butter and syrup.

Sally Simpson

Sopaipillas
Yield: 3 dozen

2 cups	flour, sifted
1 teaspoon	baking powder
1 teaspoon	salt
1 tablespoon	shortening
¾ cup	cold water
	oil

Sift dry ingredients. Cut in shortening; add water, shape into six balls. Roll each into very thin rounds. Cut in wedge shapes and fry in hot oil approximately 4 minutes, or until puffed and golden brown. Serve with honey or cinnamon/sugar mixture.

Mitzi Rowe

Funnel Cakes
Yields: 6

2½ cups	flour
1 teaspoon	baking powder
¼ teaspoon	salt
¼ teaspoon	cinnamon
2	eggs
2 cups	milk
	oil
	powdered sugar

Sift flour, baking powder, salt and cinnamon together. Beat eggs; add milk and combine with flour mixture. Beat until smooth. Pour ⅓ to ½ cup into a large funnel, holding your finger over the spout. Release, spiraling batter into 2 inches of hot oil in a heavy skillet. Lightly brown one side; turn. Drain on paper towels. Sprinkle with powdered sugar. Serve immediately. Also good served with hot maple syrup.

Lou Baughman

Parmesan Biscuits
Serves: 4

¼ cup	butter or margarine
	Parmesan cheese, grated
1 can	refrigerated biscuits

Melt butter in an 8-inch round or square pan. Sprinkle Parmesan cheese to cover melted butter. Cut each biscuit into quarters. Coat each quarter with cheese-butter mixture and place in pan, sides touching. Bake at 450 degrees F. for 6-8 minutes. Turn out onto serving plate while hot.

René Westerfeld

Blueberry Muffins

Yield: 1 dozen

½ cup	butter
1 cup	sugar
2	eggs
1 teaspoon	vanilla
2 cups	flour
2 teaspoons	baking powder
½ teaspoon	salt
½ cup	milk
2½ cups	fresh blueberries
2 teaspoons	sugar

On low speed, cream butter and sugar until fluffy. Add eggs one at a time, beating after each addition. Add vanilla and mix until blended. Sift dry ingredients together. Add alternately with milk. Mash ½ cup berries and stir in by hand. Add rest of blueberries whole and stir. Grease muffin tins, including top surface. Pile mix high in each muffin cup. Sprinkle sugar over tops. Bake at 375 degrees F. for 30 minutes. Cool in pan at least 30 minutes before removing.

Dixie Aftonomos

Apple Muffins

Yield: 18

1½ cups	brown sugar, packed
⅔ cup	oil
1	egg
1 cup	sour milk or buttermilk
1 teaspoon	baking soda
1 teaspoon	salt
1 teaspoon	vanilla
2½ cups	flour
1½ cups	apples, diced
½ cup	pecans, chopped
⅓ cup	sugar
1 teaspoon	butter or margarine, melted

Combine first 3 ingredients. In a separate bowl combine buttermilk, soda, salt and vanilla. Combine two mixtures. Add flour; mix well. Fold in apples and pecans. Pour into muffin papers and sprinkle ⅓ cup sugar combined with 1 teaspoon melted butter. Bake at 325 degrees F. for 30 minutes.

Darlene Raim

Nutty Apple Raisin Loaf

Yield: 2 loaves

3	eggs
1½ cups	oil
3 medium	apples, pared and chopped
1½ teaspoons	vanilla
2 cups	sugar
1½ cups	whole wheat flour
1¾ cups	unbleached white flour
2 teaspoons	baking soda
1 teaspoon	baking powder
1 teaspoon	salt
1 teaspoon	cinnamon
1 teaspoon	ground cloves
½ teaspoon	allspice
¼ cup	water
1 cup	raisins
⅔ cup	nuts, chopped

Preheat oven to 350 degrees F. Grease and flour two 8½ x 4½ inch loaf pans. Beat together eggs, oil, apples, sugar and vanilla. Add all other ingredients except raisins and nuts. Mix until moistened. Stir in raisins and nuts. Pour into prepared pans. Bake at 350 degrees F. for 55-60 minutes or until bread tests done. Cool to serve.

Suzanne Seemann

Pumpkin Bread

3 cups	sugar
1 cup	salad oil
3	eggs
2 cups	pumpkin
3 cups	flour
½ teaspoon	baking powder
½ teaspoon	salt
1 teaspoon	soda
1 teaspoon	cinnamon
1 teaspoon	ground cloves
1 teaspoon	nutmeg
½ cup	pecans, chopped (optional)

Preheat oven to 350 degrees F. Mix ingredients in order listed. Place in two 9 x 9 x 2 inch loaf pans and bake for 1 hour. Serve with cream cheese.

Caroline Maney

Zucchini Bread

1 cup	unpeeled zucchini, grated
1 cup	sugar
1	egg
½ cup	oil
1½ cups	flour
1 teaspoon	cinnamon
½ teaspoon	salt
½ teaspoon	baking soda
½ teaspoon	nutmeg
¼ teaspoon	baking powder
¼ teaspoon	grated lemon peel
½ cup	nuts, chopped

Combine zucchini, sugar, egg and oil; mix well. Add the remaining ingredients and stir. Pour into a greased loaf pan. Bake 60-65 minutes at 325 degrees F. Cool for 10 minutes before removing from pan. Remove and cool thoroughly. Wrap in foil and store overnight.

Linda Schambeau

Strawberry Bread

Yield: 2 loaves

2 (10 ounce) packages	frozen strawberries
4	eggs
1 ¼ cups	oil
3 cups	flour
2 cups	sugar
1 teaspoon	baking soda
1 teaspoon	salt
3 teaspoons	cinnamon
1 cup	nuts, chopped

Stir thawed strawberries, eggs and oil together. Mix dry ingredients and add to the strawberry mixture. Stir until blended. Add nuts and mix well. Pour into 2 greased and floured loaf pans. Bake at 350 degrees F. for 1 hour.

Dinah Remington

Basic Quick Sweet Dough

¾ cup	milk
½ cup	sugar
1 ¼ teaspoons	salt
½ cup	margarine
⅓ cup	warm (105-115 degrees F.) water
2 packages	yeast
3	eggs, room temperature
5½-6 cups	flour

Scald milk; stir in sugar, salt and margarine. Cool to lukewarm. Pour warm water into warmed bowl. Sprinkle in yeast and stir until dissolved. Add lukewarm milk mixture, eggs and 5 cups flour. Mix with dough hooks or mix by hand until well blended, about 3 minutes. Add remaining flour ½ cup at a time as needed. Knead until smooth and elastic. Place dough in a greased bowl, turning to grease top. Cover and let rise in a warm place free from draft until doubled in size, about 1 hour. Punch down and divide dough for rolls or coffee cakes as desired.

Suzanne Seemann

Yummy Pecan Rolls
Yield: 2 dozen

1	basic sweet dough recipe
1½ cups	brown sugar
¾ cup	syrup
6 tablespoons	butter or margarine, softened
1 cup	pecans, chopped
4 tablespoons	butter or margarine, softened
½ cup	sugar
1 tablespoon	cinnamon

Combine brown sugar, syrup, and butter in a saucepan and heat until sugar is dissolved. Bring to a rolling boil for 1 minute. Pour into two 11 x 7 x 1½ inch pans. Sprinkle with pecans. On a lightly floured board divide dough in half. Roll each section into a 12 x 9 rectangle. Brush with butter and sprinkle with cinnamon and sugar. Roll up tightly, jellyroll style, beginning with long side. Seal by pinching ends. Cut into 12 one-inch slices; place cut-side down over syrup-pecan mixture. Cover and allow to rise in a warm place until almost doubled, about 30 minutes. Bake in a preheated 375 degree F. oven for 25 minutes. Turn out onto 2 large platters.

Suzanne Seemann

Profiteroles (Cream Puffs)

1 cup	water
½ cup	butter or margarine
1 cup	flour
¼ teaspoon	salt
4	eggs

Heat butter and water in a pan until butter is melted. Reduce heat. Add flour and salt. Using wooden spoon, stir and beat until mixture leaves sides of pan and forms a smooth ball. Remove from heat. Add unbeaten eggs one at a time, stirring vigorously after each addition. Mixture will be thick and shiny. Drop on cookie sheet by rounded teaspoon. Bake at 400 degrees F. for 30 minutes.

Lesley Blalock

Cranberry Bread

Yield: 1 loaf

2 cups	flour
½ teaspoon	salt
1½ teaspoons	baking powder
½ teaspoon	baking soda
1 cup	sugar
1	egg, beaten
½ cup	orange juice
2 tablespoons	hot water
2 tablespoons	shortening, melted
1 cup	fresh cranberries, chopped
½ cup	pecans, chopped
	rind of 1 orange, grated (optional)

Sift dry ingredients together. Add egg, orange juice, hot water and melted shortening. Combine until all ingredients are moistened. Fold in cranberries, nuts and orange rind. Pour into a greased loaf pan lined with waxed paper. Bake at 325 degrees F. for 1 hour and 10 minutes. Cool thoroughly and place in refrigerator. Slice and serve cold.

Betty Sahm

Banana Bread

Yield: 1 loaf

½ cup	butter or margarine, softened
1 cup	whole wheat flour
½ cup	flour
¾ cup	brown sugar
1	egg
1 teaspoon	baking soda
¾ teaspoon	salt
1¼ cups	banana, mashed
¼ cup	plain yogurt

Combine all ingredients in a large mixing bowl. Pour into a greased 9 x 5 x 3 inch loaf pan and bake at 350 degrees F. for 40-45 minutes or until toothpick inserted comes out clean.

Christine Watson

Sunshine Bread

Yield: 1 loaf

½ cup	dried apricots
1 medium	orange
2 tablespoons	butter
1½ cups	sugar
1 teaspoon	vanilla
1	egg
2 cups	flour, sifted
2 teaspoons	baking powder
¼ teaspoon	baking soda
½ teaspoon	salt
¾ cup	nuts, chopped

Soak apricots in enough cold water to cover for ½ hour. Squeeze juice from orange into a measuring cup and add enough boiling water to make 1 cup. Put orange skins and drained apricots through a food processor or blender. Cream butter and sugar, add vanilla, egg and fruit mixture. Beat until smooth. Add dry ingredients alternately with orange juice and water mixture, blending after each addition. Stir in nuts. Bake at 350 degrees F. for 1 hour in a greased and floured 9 x 5 inch pan.

Suzanne Seemann

Parmesan Sticks

1	loaf bread
4 sticks	butter
8 ounces	Parmesan cheese, grated
	paprika

Remove crusts from bread and cut into 4 or 5 thin strips. Melt butter one stick at a time in saucepan. Soak bread sticks in butter, roll in Parmesan cheese and place on cookie sheet. Sprinkle with paprika. Bake 10 minutes at 400 degrees F. Store in an airtight container.

Dinah Remington

Eggs Cheese & Pasta

Eggs, Cheese and Pasta

Eggs MacDonald

Serves: 4

A vegetarian's original version of eggs benedict.

1½ tablespoons	butter or margarine
1½ tablespoons	flour
¾ cup	milk
¾ cup (3 ounces)	Cheddar cheese, shredded
	salt
	pepper
4	eggs
2 tablespoons	water
2 tablespoons	butter or margarine, divided
4	tomato slices, cut
	¼-inch thick
4 slices	toast, buttered
	chopped parsley (optional)

Melt butter in a heavy saucepan over low heat. Add flour, stirring until smooth. Cook 1 minute, stirring constantly. Gradually add milk and cook over medium heat, stirring until thickened and bubbly. Add cheese, ⅛ teaspoon salt and a dash of pepper, stirring until smooth. Set aside. Combine eggs, water, ¼ teaspoon salt and a dash of pepper; beat well with a fork. Melt 1 tablespoon of butter in a 10-inch skillet. Add egg mixture and cook over low heat until eggs are partially set. Stir occasionally until the eggs are firm but still moist. Fry tomato slices in remaining 1 tablespoon butter, 1 minute on each side. Place a tomato slice on each piece of toast. Spoon eggs over tomato and top with cheese sauce. Garnish with parsley.

G.C. MacDonald

Marvelous Marv's Mexican Medley

Serves: 6

2 medium	onions, chopped
2-3 cloves	garlic, finely minced
1	green pepper, chopped
4 tablespoons	butter or margarine
1 (11 ounce) can	Cheddar cheese soup
1 (10¾ ounce) can	cream of mushroom soup
¾ cup	enchilada sauce (canned)
1 (4 ounce) can	green chilies, chopped
1	tomato, chopped
3 ounces	sherry
1 pound	sausage, cooked and drained
2½ cups	chicken, cooked and chopped
½ teaspoon	cayenne pepper
½ teaspoon	cumin
	salt to taste
1-2 cups	Monterey Jack cheese, shredded
1-2 cups	Longhorn Cheddar cheese, grated
6 large	flour tortillas, warmed
6	eggs, soft scrambled
	sour cream
	Cheddar cheese, grated

Sauté onions, garlic and green pepper in butter until tender. Add next 11 ingredients. Simmer 20-30 minutes. Add cheeses and stir until melted. Place 3 tablespoons of scrambled eggs in the center of each tortilla and top with 3 tablespoons of sauce. Roll each tortilla and place seam-side down on individual plates. Cover with 5-6 tablespoons of sauce. Top each of the plates with a dollop of sour cream and additional grated cheese. Place under the broiler or in a microwave to melt the cheese.

Marvin DeBolt

Baked Eggs Supreme

Serves: 6-8

Great for those special breakfasts or for brunch.

2 cups	Cheddar cheese, grated
¼ cup	margarine, cut into small pieces
½ teaspoon	salt
¼ teaspoon	pepper
2 teaspoons	prepared mustard
1 cup	Half and Half
12	eggs, slightly beaten

Grease a 2½ quart casserole. Place cheese on bottom of casserole, dot with the margarine. Mix the seasonings with the cream. Pour one half of this mixture over the cheese; pour eggs over the cream mixture. Do not stir. Pour remaining cream mixture over the eggs and do not stir. Bake at 325 degrees F. for 50 minutes or until eggs are set.

René Westerfeld

Chili Rellenos Casserole

Serves: 4-6

1 cup	Half and Half
2	eggs
⅓ cup	flour
3 (4 ounce) cans	whole green chilies
½ pound	Monterey Jack cheese, grated
½ pound	sharp Cheddar cheese, grated
1 (8 ounce) can	tomato sauce

Beat Half and Half with eggs and flour until smooth. Split chilies, rinse out seeds and drain. Mix cheeses. Reserve ⅓ cup for topping. Make alternate layers of remaining cheese, chilies and egg mixture in a deep 1½ quart casserole dish. Pour tomato sauce over the top and sprinkle with reserved cheese. Bake at 350 degrees F. for 1¼ hours or until done in the center.

Catherine Rogers

Sunrise Egg Casserole
Serves: 10

Serve with a fresh fruit cup, baked ham, bacon or sausage.

1 pound	fresh mushrooms, sliced
4 tablespoons	butter
14	hard boiled eggs, cut into quarters
1 (10 ounce) package	tiny garden peas
1 (8 ounce) can	water chestnuts, sliced and drained
1 (10¾ ounce) can	cream of chicken soup
1 cup	sour cream
1 teaspoon	onion, minced
¼ cup	sherry
3 tablespoons	pimento
	salt and pepper to taste
1 cup	buttered bread crumbs

Sauté mushrooms in butter until tender. Arrange the mushrooms, eggs, peas and water chestnuts in layers in that order in a 9 x 13 x 2 inch casserole. In a medium saucepan mix and heat the soup, sour cream and onion. Add the sherry, pimento, salt and pepper. Pour mixture evenly over the layers in the casserole. Top with bread crumbs. Bake at 375 degrees F. for 20-25 minutes or just until sauce bubbles. Eggs will toughen when overcooked.

Lesley Blalock

Company's Coming For Breakfast

Serves: 10-12

This may be prepared in advance and frozen. Thaw before baking. For easy clean-up afterwards, pour into individual-size, disposable, foil loaf pans. Serve with scrambled eggs.

1 pound	mild ground pork sausage
1 pound	hot or spicy ground pork sausage
½ cup	onion, chopped
½ cup	apple, peeled and chopped
2	eggs, beaten
½ cup	milk
1½ cups	Saltine cracker crumbs
1 (17 ounce) can	apricot halves, drained and chopped

Preheat oven to 350 degrees F. Brown sausage in skillet. Add onion and apple and sauté. Drain well. Mix sausage mixture with remaining ingredients in a medium bowl. Pour into greased and floured casserole. Bake 45 minutes.

Jane Davis

Chili Cheese Pie

Serves: 6

1 (4 ounce) can	green chilies, drained, reserve liquid
1 cup	Cheddar cheese, grated
1 cup	Swiss cheese, grated
1	egg

Grease an 8 x 8 inch pan. Spread chopped green chilies in pan. Sprinkle Cheddar and then Swiss cheese over the chilies. Mix juice from chilies with egg and drizzle over cheese. Bake at 350 degrees F. for 25 minutes. Let set before cutting into squares.

Cut into small squares and serve as appetizers or use as a side dish with roast.

Kathy Wile

Overnight Breakfast Casserole

Serves: 6-8

Breakfast entertaining is a breeze when the main dish is prepared the night before.

6 slices	bread, trimmed and cubed
1 pound	sausage, cooked and drained
¼ cup	green pepper, chopped
1 (4 ounce) can	mushrooms, drained
1 cup (4 ounces)	Cheddar cheese, grated
6	eggs
2 cups	milk
1 teaspoon	salt
¼ teaspoon	pepper

Layer ingredients in a 13 x 9 x 2 inch casserole in the following order: bread cubes, cooked sausage, green pepper, mushrooms and cheese. Beat together eggs, milk, salt and pepper and pour over layers. Cover with foil and refrigerate overnight. Bake uncovered at 350 degrees F. for 35 minutes.

Marie Johnson

Ham and Eggs Crêpes With Mushroom Sauce

Serves: 6-8

CRÊPES

1 cup	biscuit baking mix
1	egg
1 cup	milk

MUSHROOM SAUCE

½ pound	fresh mushrooms, sliced
2 tablespoons	onion, chopped

3 tablespoons	butter or margarine
1 tablespoon	flour
½ teaspoon	salt
⅛ teaspoon	ground nutmeg
⅛ teaspoon	pepper
1 cup	sour cream
⅓ cup	milk
1 teaspoon	prepared mustard
2 tablespoons	parsley, snipped

FILLING

¼ pound	cooked ham, finely chopped
2 tablespoons	butter or margarine
8	eggs
½ cup	milk
¼ cup	water
½ teaspoon	pepper

Combine all ingredients for crêpes and beat with a rotary beater until smooth. Spoon 2 tablespoons of batter into a hot, lightly greased, 6 or 7 inch skillet. Immediately rotate the skillet until batter covers the bottom. Cook until light brown, turn and brown on other side. When removing from skillet, place crêpe so that the first-cooked side is down on baking sheet or tray. Cover and keep warm.

Prepare sauce by sautéing mushrooms and onion in butter until tender or 3-5 minutes. Stir in flour, salt, nutmeg and pepper. Cook and stir over low heat until mixture is bubbly. Remove from heat. Mix sour cream, milk, mustard and parsley and stir into mushroom mixture. Heat, stirring constantly, just to boiling.

To prepare filling, cook and stir ham in butter over medium heat until light brown, about 5 minutes. Mix eggs, milk, water and pepper with fork; pour over ham in skillet. As mixture begins to set at bottom and side, gently lift cooked portions with spatula so thin, uncooked portions can flow to the bottom. Avoid constant stirring. Cook until eggs are thickened throughout but still moist, or 3-5 minutes. Spoon ¼ cup egg-ham mixture on the center of each crêpe; roll up. Place seam-side down on plate. Spoon Mushroom Sauce over the top.

Janey Rynearson

Crab Quiche

Serves: 6

½ cup	mayonnaise
2 tablespoons	flour
2	eggs, beaten
½ cup	milk
6 ounces	crabmeat, cooked
¼ pound	Cheddar cheese, shredded
¼ pound	Monterey Jack cheese, shredded
⅓ cup	green onion, chopped
1	pie shell, pre-baked

Combine mayonnaise, flour, eggs and milk. Mix thoroughly. Stir in crabmeat, cheeses and onion. Spoon into a baked pie shell and bake at 350 degrees F. for 30 to 40 minutes or until firm in center.

Swiss cheese may be substituted for the other cheeses.

René Westerfeld

Shrimp Quiche

Serves: 6

1	pie shell, pre-baked for 6 minutes
1 cup	uncooked shrimp, peeled
1 cup	Monterey Jack cheese, cubed
3 tablespoons	green onion, chopped
4	eggs
2 tablespoons	milk
2 tablespoons	parsley, chopped
	salt and pepper to taste
	Tabasco sauce to taste
½ cup	fresh mushrooms, sliced

Place shrimp, cheese and onion in bottom of pie shell. Beat eggs, milk, parsley and seasonings together. Pour over other ingredients. Sprinkle sliced mushrooms on top. Bake at 350 degrees F. for 45 minutes.

Judy Arrowsmith

Sherried Cheese Grits

Serves: 8

True Floridians serve cheese grits at fish fries.

8 cups	water
1 teaspoon	salt
2 cups	quick grits
1 (6 ounce) roll	garlic cheese
1 cup	butter
2 tablespoons	sherry
2 tablespoons	Worcestershire sauce
2 cloves	garlic, minced
dash	Tabasco sauce
	pepper
2	eggs

Bring water and salt to a boil. Slowly add grits, stirring often. Cook for 2½ minutes. While still hot, stir in all ingredients except eggs. Let cool. Preheat oven to 400 degrees F. Beat eggs and stir into grits. Bake 1 hour. Serve hot.

Judy Morris

Fettuccine Alfredo

Serves: 8

Vary this recipe by adding sautéed fresh mushrooms to the sauce. Bon Appétit!

½ cup	butter
2 cups	heavy cream
1 cup	Parmesan cheese, grated
	fresh Italian parsley, finely chopped
	white pepper
1 pound	Fettuccine noodles

Melt butter, add cream and heat thoroughly, but do not boil. Just before serving, add cheese, parsley and pepper. Cook noodles according to package directions. Drain; put back into pan in which they were cooked and toss with sauce. Serve immediately.

Judy Muller

Glorified Noodles

Serves: 8

A real man pleaser. Great with steak, veal or Italian dishes.

1 (8 ounce) package	egg noodles
1½ cups	cottage cheese
1 clove	garlic, crushed
1 teaspoon	Worcestershire sauce
1 cup	sour cream
½ cup	scallions, chopped
¼ teaspoon	Tabasco sauce
½ cup	fresh Parmesan cheese, grated

Cook noodles in salted water until tender. Drain. Combine noodles, cottage cheese, garlic, Worcestershire sauce, sour cream, scallions and Tabasco sauce. Turn into a greased casserole; sprinkle with cheese. Bake at 350 degrees F. for 25 minutes.

Cindy McLaughlin

Hay

Serves: 12

Great for a formal buffet or a casual pot luck supper. It feeds a crowd!

1 cup	butter
1 (8 ounce) package	narrow noodles
2 cups	raw rice
2 (10½ ounce) cans	onion soup
2 (10½ ounce) cans	chicken broth
2 (10½ ounce) cans	beef broth
1 teaspoon	soy sauce

Melt butter in a deep pan. Add raw noodles and toss until honey colored. Add rice and fold through noodles. Add liquids slowly and cook until absorbed or about 15-30 minutes. Place in a greased casserole. Bake at 350 degrees F. for 15 minutes covered and 15 minutes uncovered.

Margie DeBolt

Meats

Meats

Beef Wellington

Serves: 6

An elegant entrée that will get rave reviews from your family or guests.

1 (10 ounce) package	frozen patty shells

DUXELLES

1 pound	fresh mushrooms
2	shallots or white part of 2 green onions, finely chopped
½ cup	butter or margarine, divided and melted
	salt and pepper to taste
6	beef filets, cut 2 inches thick
6 tablespoons	dry sherry
	Béarnaise Sauce

Thaw patty shells and roll on a flour-dusted board to about 8 inch diameter. Stack between waxed paper sheets until ready to wrap meat. Keep chilled. To prepare Duxelles, clean mushrooms and chop in food processor until fine. Do not purée. Squeeze moisture from mushrooms with a clean dish towel. Sauté mushrooms and shallots in ¼ cup butter, stirring frequently, until liquid evaporates or about 10 minutes. Mixture will be dark. Add salt and pepper. Duxelles can be refrigerated for up to one week.

To continue preparation, sear filets in remaining butter. Transfer to a platter and pour 2 tablespoons sherry over the meat. Chill meat thoroughly. Pour remainder of sherry into frying pan. Crumble in ½ cup duxelles. Cook over low to medium heat, stirring until liquid evaporates or about 10-15 minutes. Cover and chill. Place equal amounts of chilled duxelle mixture in the center of each pastry shell. Place cold filet on top of mixture and salt lightly. Fold pastry to cover filet. Place seam-side down on a rimmed baking sheet. Cover and refrigerate for at least 1 hour or up to 24 hours. Bake uncovered at 425 degrees F. on lowest rack of oven for 10 minutes. Move to highest rack and bake for 8-10 minutes or until golden brown. Serve at once with a Béarnaise Sauce.

Marsha Laughlin

Grillades

Serves: 4-6

2 pounds	beef rounds
2 tablespoons	oil
⅓ cup	flour
⅓ cup	oil
1 cup	green onions, chopped
1 cup	green pepper, chopped
¾ cup	celery, chopped
2 cups	tomato, chopped
½ teaspoon	thyme
1 cup	water
¾ cup	red wine
	salt and pepper to taste
3	bay leaves
¼ teaspoon	Tabasco sauce
3 tablespoons	parsley, chopped

Lightly pound meat to ¼ inch thick pieces. Pat dry and cut into bite-size pieces. In large skillet, brown the beef on all sides in 2 tablespoons oil. Drain on paper towels and set aside. In skillet, combine flour and oil to make a dark roux. Add onion, green pepper and celery; sauté until tender. Add tomatoes and thyme and cook for 3 minutes. Add water and wine. Stir well and return meat; add salt, pepper, bay leaves and Tabasco. Stir and continue cooking on low heat for about 2 hours. Remove bay leaves and stir in parsley. Cool and then leave in refrigerator overnight. Warm to serve, adding more liquid if necessary.

Christine Watson

Lousiana Daube

Serves: 4-6

2 cloves	garlic, thinly sliced
2-3 pounds	boneless rump roast
½ teaspoon	pepper
2 teaspoons	salt
½ cup	flour
½ cup	oil
2 cups	onions, chopped
½ cup	celery, chopped
½ cup	green onions, chopped
¼ cup	parsley, chopped
2 cloves	garlic, chopped
2 (8 ounce) cans	tomato sauce
1 (6 ounce) can	tomato paste
4 cups	water
½ teaspoon	cayenne pepper
	spaghetti or pasta, cooked

Plug roast with 2 thinly sliced cloves of garlic. Salt and pepper roast and sear in an iron skillet. Mix flour and oil in a 4 quart casserole and microwave on HIGH 15-17 minutes to make a roux. Stir occasionally. When roux is a caramel color, stir in onions and celery. Microwave on HIGH for 5 minutes. Stir in green onions, parsley and remaining garlic. Cook on HIGH 3 minutes. Stir in tomato sauce, tomato paste, water and cayenne pepper. Add roast; cover and cook on HIGH 15 minutes. Microwave on MEDIUM 45 minutes, stirring and basting occasionally. Turn meat halfway through cooking. Serve roast and sauce over spaghetti or your favorite pasta.

Adrienne Parker

Steak Diane
Serves: 4-6

This recipe can be used with any type of beef. Serve with filets, tenderloin or even hamburger!

1½ tablespoons	butter
1½ tablespoons	flour
2 cups	brown stock or 1 (10½ ounce) can beef broth and enough water to make 2 cups
4-6	beef filets
1 tablespoon	catsup
2 tablespoons	Worcestershire sauce
½ cup	white wine
1 cup	green onions, chopped
1 cup	mushrooms, chopped

Melt butter and blend in flour. Cook and stir over low heat until browned. Add stock and bring to a boil. Cook 3-5 minutes. Reduce heat and simmer 30 minutes. Stir occasionally. Cool and refrigerate until ready to use. Cook steaks in a skillet. Add sauce to pan drippings and add catsup, Worcestershire sauce, white wine, green onions and mushrooms. Heat thoroughly. Pour over steaks and serve. If sauce is too thin, thicken with a mixture of water and cornstarch.

Pat McLean

Steak Tournedos

An inexpensive way to feed a large crowd. This can be prepared ahead of time and then grilled.

1-1½ pounds	flank steak
½ pound	bacon
1-2 (10 ounce) packages	frozen spinach
1 teaspoon	garlic salt
½ teaspoon	pepper, freshly ground
2 tablespoons	parsley, chopped
2 cups	Hollandaise sauce
¼ teaspoon	dried tarragon, crushed

Pound steak to even thickness. Cook bacon until almost done, but not crisp. Cook spinach according to package directions and drain thoroughly. Sprinkle steak with garlic salt and pepper; score steak diagonally, making diamond shaped cuts. Sprinkle with parsley and place bacon lengthwise on steak. Spread spinach on top of bacon as generously as desired. Roll up steak starting with narrow end. Skewer with wooden picks about 1 inch apart and cut into 1 inch slices with a sharp knife. Grill over medium coals for about 15 minutes or bake at 375 degrees F. for about 30 minutes. Add tarragon to Hollandaise sauce and serve with steaks.

Louise Burris

Steak Round-Up

Serves: 4

1	onion, chopped
½ pound	fresh mushrooms or
	1 (9 ounce) can
	mushrooms, sliced
3 tablespoons	butter or margarine
1 cup	seasoned bread crumbs
¼ teaspoon	thyme
¼ teaspoon	sage
dash	pepper
1 ½ pounds	round steak
	salt and pepper to taste
	flour
4 tablespoons	oil
¼ cup	water

Sauté onion and mushrooms in butter; add bread crumbs, thyme, sage and pepper. Stir well. Pound steak to tenderize and sprinkle with salt and pepper. Spread bread-crumb mixture over half of the steak. Top with remaining half of the meat and seal edges using wooden picks. Dredge in flour and brown in hot oil in skillet. Add water, cover tightly and bake at 325 degrees F. for 45 minutes or until meat is tender.

Anne Johnston

Grilled Flank Steak

Serves: 6-8

3 medium	flank steaks
⅔ cup	soy sauce
⅔ cup	salad oil
2 tablespoons	instant minced onions
6 tablespoons	red wine vinegar
4 tablespoons	chutney, chopped
¼ teaspoon	garlic powder

Combine all ingredients for marinade. Pour over steaks and marinate 6 hours, turning occasionally. Cook steaks on a grill over hot coals, 5 minutes per side for rare. Carve thin, diagonal slices to serve.

Linda Scoville

Sugar-Fired Beef

Serves: 10-12

1 (6 pound)	eye of round or tenderloin beef roast
¼ cup	Worcestershire sauce
2 teaspoons	sugar
2 ounces	whiskey
pinch	ground ginger
1 clove	garlic, minced
½ teaspoon	pepper
¼ cup	salt
¼ cup	powdered sugar

Combine Worcestershire sauce, sugar, whiskey, ginger, garlic and pepper. Pour over roast and marinate for 2 hours. Remove from marinade and roll in a mixture of salt and powdered sugar. Broil over a low charcoal fire for 45 minutes. The outside will be charred but the inside will remain juicy.

Shirley Grace

Sicilian Meatloaf

Serves: 6

2	eggs, beaten
¾ cup	dry bread crumbs
½ cup	tomato juice
1 clove	garlic, minced
½ teaspoon	oregano
1½ teaspoons	parsley, minced
½ teaspoon	salt
¼ teaspoon	pepper
2 pounds	ground chuck
½ pound	ham, thinly sliced
1½ cups	Mozzarella cheese, grated

Combine all ingredients except ham and cheese. Pat onto waxed paper to a 12 x 10 inch rectangle. Place sliced ham on mixture and cover with 1 cup cheese. Roll up like a jellyroll. Seal edges; place in a roaster seam-side down. Bake at 350 degrees F. for 1 hour and 15 minutes. Add remaining cheese to top and bake for 5 more minutes. Let stand 10 minutes; slice and serve.

Margie DeBolt

Oven Beef Stew
Serves: 6

Prepare this in the morning and bake in the afternoon while running errands. This can also be prepared well in advance and frozen. Thaw and heat to warm.

2½ pounds	stew meat, cubed
1 (28 ounce) can	tomatoes, undrained
1½ cups	celery, chopped
4	carrots, sliced
3	onions, sliced
1 (10 ounce) package	frozen corn
1 (10 ounce) package	frozen peas
4 tablespoons	quick cooking tapioca
2 cubes	beef flavored bouillon
1 tablespoon	sugar
1 tablespoon	pepper
⅛ teaspoon	thyme
⅛ teaspoon	rosemary
⅛ teaspoon	marjoram
¼-½ cup	red wine
1 package	dried onion soup mix
	salt to taste

Combine all ingredients except salt in a 5 quart casserole. Cover and cook at 250 degrees F. for 5 hours. Stir after 3½ hours and add salt.

Carol DeBolt

Veal Normandy   *Serves: 6*

2 pounds	veal scallops (12 slices)
	salt, pepper and garlic
	powder to taste
	flour
4 tablespoons	butter
¼ cup	cognac
4	apples, peeled and sliced
2 tablespoons	cinnamon and sugar mixture
2 tablespoons	green onion, chopped
1½ cups	apple juice
1 cup	cream
½ cup	sour cream

Season veal scallops with salt, pepper and garlic powder. Dust with flour and sauté in butter until meat loses its pinkness. Heat the cognac in a brandy warmer; ignite and pour over the meat. When flame is out, remove veal to an ovenproof platter. Using the same pan in which the meat was cooked, sauté the apples, cinnamon and sugar mixture and green onions until apples are firm but tender, or about 10 minutes. Add apple juice and increase heat to high to reduce the juice to half. Lower the heat and stir in cream and sour cream. Pour apple mixture evenly over the veal and warm in the oven.

May be made in advance. To serve, bring to room temperature and then warm slowly in the oven. Great served with rice!

Veal Boursin   *Serves: 4*

8 (⅛ inch) thick	veal scallops
	salt, pepper and garlic
	powder to taste
	flour
8 ounces	Boursin cheese
8 slices	bacon

Season veal scallops with salt, pepper, garlic powder, and dust with flour. Place 1 ounce Boursin on each scallop and roll up. Spiral 1 slice of bacon around each scallopo, and fasten with a toothpick. Sauté scallops for several minutes on each side; when bacon is crisp, scallops are done. Do not overcook. Cheese will be softened. Serve at once! Marvelous with mushrooms sauteéd in butter.

Veal Oscar

Serves: 2

8 ounces	milk-fed veal, pounded very thin
2 cups	flour, seasoned with salt and pepper
2 tablespoons	butter
8 ounces	Alaskan King Crab meat
8 ounces	asparagus
	Bordelaise Sauce

Pound veal medallions very thin. Veal is then dredged in seasoned flour. Use a black skillet to melt 2 tablespoons of butter and allow butter to brown before placing veal in skillet. Allow each piece of veal to cook in pan for 45-50 SECONDS on each side. Remove veal from skillet to oven pan to keep warm until sauces are ready. Arrange each serving of Veal Oscar in oven pan and later on serving plate as follows: Place medallions side-by-side in pan or plate. On top of veal place 1 finger (1½-2 ounces) of crab. Next to finger of crab place finger of green asparagus. Then repeat crab and asparagus sequence. Cover with Sauce Béarnaise and brown under the broiler. To serve, place 2 tablespoons Sauce Bordelaise on a serving plate and top with veal covered with Sauce Béarnaise.

Sauce Béarnaise

6-8 tablespoons	butter
4	egg yolks
1 teaspoon	lemon juice
4 tablespoons	white wine
1 shot	Worcestershire sauce
1 shot	Tabasco sauce
2	shallots
dash	chervil, flaked
dash	parsley, flaked
dash	tarragon
dash	cider vinegar
dash	salt
dash	pepper

Melt 2 tablespoons butter and set aside. In a stainless bowl, place, but do not mix, egg yolks, lemon juice, 2 tablespoons white wine, salt and pepper. Set aside. In a second pan, melt 2-3 tablespoons additional butter and sauté shallots. Add to shallots, chervil, parsley, 2 tablespoons white wine, tarragon and vinegar. Simmer until reduced; set aside. In a double boiler, bring water in bottom pan to a boil and in top place egg yolks, lemon juice, and white wine from first saucepan. Whip mixture until frothy; remove from heat, beating until cool. Take melted butter that was set aside and drizzle into whipped yolk mixture. Add shallot mixture. This results in a thick, yellow sauce with a primary tarragon flavor.

Sauce Bordelaise

2 cans	commercial beef bouillon
4-6 ounces	hearty red wine
4 tablespoons	butter
4 tablespoons	flour
2	shallots
40	peppercorns
4	bay leaves

In one of two small saucepans, place 2 tablespoons of butter and sauté shallots,-bay leaves and peppercorns. Add wine and cook down to almost dry; remove from heat and set aside. In second saucepan, melt 2 tablespoons butter; add flour, mix and let cook slowly; do not burn. Add bouillon stock, then add reduced mixture from first saucepan. Let simmer 10 minutes. Strain with a sieve and set aside.

Mark D. Pearson
Executive Chef
Sandestin Beach Resort

Saltimbocca

Serves: 4

1 pound	top round veal, cut into 4 pieces ½ inch thick
4 thin	slices proscuitto
4 slices	Monterey Jack cheese
½ teaspoon	ground sage
	flour
2 tablespoons	olive oil
1 cup	mushrooms, sliced
2 teaspoons	shallots, chopped
1 cup	dry white wine

Pound each veal slice to ⅛ inch thick. Cover each with a slice of proscuitto and then with a slice of cheese. Trim each slice to fit; sprinkle with sage. Roll each piece of veal jellyroll fashion and secure with toothpicks. Sprinkle lightly with flour and brown on all sides in olive oil. Add mushrooms, shallots and wine. Cover and cook on low heat until tender or about 10 minutes. Remove meat to a platter and keep warm. Boil sauce remaining in pan uncovered until reduced to desired consistency or about 5 minutes.

Linda Carr

Marinated Veal Roast

Serves: 8

½ cup	soy sauce
2 tablespoons	artificial sweetener
3 teaspoons	sugar
	salt and pepper to taste
¼ teaspoon	garlic powder
1 (4 pound)	veal roast

Combine all ingredients except veal roast. Place roast in marinade mixture for at least 1½ hours. Turn frequently. Place veal in an uncovered baking dish and bake at 350 degrees F. for 2 hours or until meat thermometer indicates doneness. Baste veal with marinade while baking.

Ginny Glynn Barr

Lamb Kabobs

Serves: 8

1	leg of lamb, boned and cut into 1 inch cubes
½ cup	olive oil
4 tablespoons	lemon juice
1 teaspoon	salt
¼ teaspoon	pepper
	oregano
	green pepper slices
	onion wedges
	fresh mushrooms
	cherry tomatoes
	small new potatoes

Place lamb in a bowl. Combine oil, lemon juice, salt and pepper and pour over lamb. Marinate for at least 3 hours. Thread lamb and vegetables onto skewers. Grill over glowing coals until done. Sprinkle with oregano.

Sally Simpson

Surf and Turf Kabob Sauce

Yield: 3½ cups

Good on beef or fish!

1½ cups	salad oil
¾ cup	soy sauce
¼ cup	Worcestershire sauce
2 tablespoons	dry mustard
2½ teaspoons	salt
1½ teaspoons	parsley flakes
1 tablespoon	fresh ground pepper
½ cup	wine vinegar
1 clove	garlic, crushed (optional)
½ cup	lemon juice

Blend all ingredients in a blender for 30-40 seconds. Store tightly covered in refrigerator until ready to use. Marinate desired meat for at least 2-3 hours before cooking.

Judy O'Steen

Maple Grilled Pork Chops *Serves: 4*

1 cup	catsup
1 cup	maple syrup
¾ cup	dry white wine
¼ cup	water
1 teaspoon	instant beef bouillon granules
1	bay leaf
2 cloves	garlic, minced
¼ teaspoon	ground ginger
1 teaspoon	dried thyme, crushed
1 teaspoon	dried basil, crushed
½ teaspoon	chili powder
½ teaspoon	dry mustard
½ teaspoon	salt
¼ teaspoon	pepper
⅛ teaspoon	ground cloves
4	pork loin chops, cut 1½ inches thick

Combine all ingredients except chops in a saucepan and bring to a boil. Reduce heat and simmer, uncovered, for 30 minutes or until sauce is reduced to 2 cups. Stir occasionally while cooking. Grill chops over medium coals for 20 minutes. Turn chops and grill 10-15 minutes more. Brush sauce over chops occasionally while grilling.

Donna Bridgford

Pirate's Pork Tenderloin   *Serves: 6*

Serve with Seaside Stuffed Squash.

6 slices	bacon, diced
⅓ cup	onion, chopped
1 (4 ounce) can	mushrooms, sliced, reserve liquid
1 pound	pork tenderloin, cut into ½ inch thick pieces
	salt and pepper to taste
2	eggs, beaten
2 cups	Italian bread crumbs

Fry bacon in a skillet; remove and sauté onion and mushrooms. Combine bacon, onion and mushrooms and set aside. Sprinkle pork with salt and pepper. Dip pieces into egg and then into bread crumbs. Brown in skillet. Fill a 1 quart casserole with alternate layers of meat, then vegetables and bacon, and top with meat. Pour reserved mushroom liquid over the meat. Seal casserole tightly with foil; bake 30 minutes at 350 degrees F.

Elaine Doolin

Hot Honda Barbeque Sauce   *Yield: 1 ½ gallons*

Excellent on beef or pork!

2 (24 ounce) bottles	catsup
½ cup	margarine
1 (10 ounce) bottle	Worcestershire sauce
¼ cup	brown sugar
¼ cup	lemon juice
dash	Tabasco sauce

Heat catsup in a large Dutch oven. Add remaining ingredients and bring to a boil Cool. This may be stored in the refrigerator or sealed in canning jars.

Bill and Buddy Chambless

129

Holiday Pork Roast

Serves: 10-12

1 (5 pound)	pork roast, boned, rolled and tied
2 tablespoons	dry mustard
2 teaspoons	thyme
½ cup	soy sauce
½ cup	sherry
2 cloves	garlic, minced
1 teaspoon	ginger

Rub roast with a mixture of mustard and thyme. Mix remaining mustard with soy sauce, sherry, garlic and ginger and pour over roast. Let stand at room temperature for 3-4 hours or overnight in the refrigerator. Turn roast occasionally. Remove meat from marinade and place on grill in a shallow baking pan. Cook, uncovered, at 350 degrees F. for 2½-3 hours. Baste occasionally with marinade. Serve with Currant Sauce.

Currant Sauce

1 (10 ounce) jar	currant jelly
1 tablespoon	soy sauce
2 tablespoons	sherry

Melt currant jelly. Add soy sauce and sherry and simmer 2-3 minutes.

Mary Mathews

Herbed Pork Roast

Serves: 4-6

1 (4-5 pound)	pork loin boneless roast
	olive oil
	salt and pepper
	dried thyme
	oregano
	caraway seeds
	flour
1 medium	onion, thinly sliced
¾ cup	dry white wine
1½ cups	chicken broth
⅛ teaspoon	ground nutmeg
1 clove	garlic, minced

Rub roast lightly with oil. Sprinkle salt, pepper, thyme, oregano and caraway seeds on roast and pat lightly with flour so spices will adhere. Fasten onion slices all over roast with wooden picks. Wrap in foil or plastic wrap and let stand in refrigerator for 6-12 hours. Mix wine and broth and cook for 5 minutes. Add garlic and nutmeg. Keep sauce warm and baste roast as it cooks. To cook roast, bake at 325 degrees F. for about 35 minutes per pound.

Bobbie Pennington

Pork Chops And Wild Rice

Serves: 8

8 large	pork chops
	flour
	salt and pepper to taste
4 tablespoons	butter or margarine, melted
8	onion slices
8	tomato slices
8	green pepper slices
1 (6 ounce) box	wild rice
2 (10½ ounce) cans	beef consommé
	tomato juice (optional)

Flour, salt and pepper pork chops. Brown in melted butter. Drain and place pork chops in a 9 x 13 x 2 inch roasting pan. Top each chop with an onion slice, tomato slice and green pepper slice. Sprinkle rice mix over chops and add the consommé. Cover and bake at 350 degrees F. for 1½ hours. If more liquid is needed, add tomato juice.

Jeanne Caperton

Indoor-Outdoor Marinade

Yield: 2 cups

1 envelope	dry onion soup mix
¼ cup	sugar
1 cup	catsup
1 cup	water
½ cup	vinegar
½ cup	salad oil
2 tablespoons	prepared mustard
2 slices	lemon
½ teaspoon	salt

Combine all ingredients in a 1½ quart glass container. Microwave 5 minutes on HIGH, then 5 minutes more on MEDIUM. Cool completely. Pour over meat and marinate in refrigerator for 24 hours.

Sally Simpson

Italian Sausage And Peppers

Serves: 6

2 pounds	Italian link sausage, cut into 2 inch pieces
1 large	green pepper, sliced
1 large	onion, sliced
½ cup	water
1 (16 ounce) can	tomato sauce
1 (6 ounce) can	tomato paste
½ cup	water
1 tablespoon	chili powder
½ teaspoon	garlic powder
1-2 tablespoons	Italian seasoning
1 teaspoon	lemon pepper
¼ teaspoon	oregano
2	bay leaves
1 teaspoon	salt
1-2 teaspoons	sugar
1 (12 ounce) package	Italian noodles, cooked and drained

Combine sausage, green pepper and onions in a large pot and cook over medium heat until sausage is browned. Drain grease. Add remaining ingredients except noodles. Stir well, cover and cook over low heat for approximately 30 minutes. Serve over noodles.

Debi Roberts

German Feast

5 medium	potatoes, approximately 1¾ pounds
½ pound	smoked knackwurst
½ pound	smoked bratwurst
1½ cups	dry white wine
6 tablespoons	olive oil
3 teaspoons	fresh thyme, snipped or 1 teaspoon dried thyme
1½ teaspoons	fresh tarragon, snipped or ½ teaspoon dried tarragon
1½ teaspoons	fresh marjoram, snipped or ½ teaspoon dried marjoram
1 tablespoon	shallots, minced
1 tablespoon	white wine tarragon vinegar
¼ teaspoon	Dijon mustard
1	egg yolk
1 tablespoon	fresh parsley, snipped
1 tablespoon	fresh chives, snipped
½ teaspoon	salt
¼ teaspoon	white pepper

Cook potatoes in boiling water to cover in a Dutch oven until just tender or about 22 minutes. Drain; cool slightly; peel and cut into ¼ inch slices. Keep warm. Pierce sausages with a fork. Combine sausages, wine, 4 tablespoons of the oil, thyme, tarragon and marjoram in a large skillet; simmer partially covered, turning sausages frequently for 10 minutes. Reserve sausages and wine mixture separately. Sauté shallots in 1 tablespoon of the oil in a small saucepan until soft or about 2 minutes. Add reserved wine mixture; heat to boiling. Simmer until reduced to ¾ cup or about 10 minutes. Stir in vinegar and mustard. Remove from heat. Gradually whisk wine mixture into egg yolk in small bowl. Stir in half the parsley, half the chives, salt and pepper, and pour over potatoes. Cover. Cut sausages into ½ inch slices. Brown in remaining oil in large skillet. Arrange potato mixture and sausages in serving bowl. Sprinkle with remaining parsley and chives.

Caroline Maney

Venison Stew

Serves: 4

A good hunter's stew! Serve over noodles.

2 pounds	venison
¼ cup	flour
1 teaspoon	salt
	pepper to taste
3 tablespoons	oil
1 stalk	celery, chopped
3 onions	sliced
1 tablespoon	Worcestershire sauce
2 cups	tomatoes

Cut venison into serving size pieces. Mix flour, salt and pepper. Coat venison with flour mixture. Heat oil in skillet and brown venison on all sides. Add celery, onion, Worcestershire sauce and tomatoes and cook, covered, for 1-2 hours (depending on age of animal) or until tender.

Maurice McLaughlin

Venison Teriyaki

Serves: 4-6

A quick, easy way to prepare venison!

	tenderloin of venison
½ cup	butter, melted
1 teaspoon	basil
1 teaspoon	thyme
1-2 teaspoons	marjoram
½ cup	teriyaki sauce
¾-1 cup	Burgundy wine

Slice tenderloin in ½ inch thick slices. Combine remaining ingredients in a saucepan and bring to a boil. Add venison slices and cook to desired doneness. Serve over wild rice or brown rice.

Judy Arrowsmith

Venison Chili

Serves: 6-8

2 pounds	venison, cut into ½ inch cubes
1 pound	ground pork
1 large	onion, chopped
4 cloves	garlic, minced
3 tablespoons	water
3	bay leaves
1 quart	ripe tomatoes or 1 (28 ounce) can tomatoes
6 tablespoons	chili powder
1 tablespoon	flour
1 tablespoon	dried oregano
1 tablespoon	salt
1 tablespoon	cumin

Combine venison, pork, onion, garlic, water and bay leaves in a large saucepan; cover and steam for 5 minutes. Rub tomatoes through a colander and add to meat. Mix chili powder with flour. Stir into the meat mixture. Cook and stir for 20 minutes. Add oregano, salt and cumin; cook over low heat, covered, for 2 hours. If necessary, add more water. Serve over red beans or rice or both!

Tena McLaughlin

Poultry

Poultry

Artichoke Chicken   *Serves: 4*

Try this when you need an easy but elegant dish for a "spur of the moment" dinner get-together.

1 cup	flour
½ teaspoon	garlic salt
¼ teaspoon	pepper
4	chicken breasts
4 tablespoons	butter
3 tablespoons	vegetable oil
½ cup	onion, minced
1 (10½ ounce) can	chicken broth
1 cup	mushrooms, sliced
1 (16 ounce) can	artichoke hearts
1 cup	sauterne

Mix flour, garlic salt and pepper. Dredge chicken breasts in flour mixture. Brown in butter and oil. Add onion and sauté. Add broth and simmer for 20 minutes. Add mushrooms, artichoke hearts and sauterne. Simmer for 10 minutes. Serve over yellow rice.

Lou Baughman

Chicken Dijon   *Serves: 12*

6 whole	chicken breasts, halved
	salt and pepper to taste
	garlic powder to taste
1½ cups	sour cream
1½ cups	Dijon mustard
2 cups	Italian bread crumbs

Sprinkle chicken with salt, pepper and garlic. Combine sour cream and mustard. Dip each chicken breast in the mustard mixture, coating well, then dredge in the bread crumbs. Arrange chicken in a single layer in a microwave-safe baking dish. Microwave at HIGH 12 minutes. Rotate dish ½ turn and microwave 12 more minutes.

Nancy Reichstetter

Spinach-Chicken Soufflé Roll

Serves: 8

Prepare in advance and freeze. When ready to serve, thaw. Bake at 375 degrees F. for 30 minutes, then add cheese triangles and melt under the broiler.

4 tablespoons	butter
½ cup	flour
2 cups	milk
½ cup	Parmesan cheese, grated
½ cup	Cheddar cheese, grated
¼ teaspoon	salt
4	egg yolks, slightly beaten
4	egg whites, room temperature
	Spinach-Chicken Filling
4 slices	American cheese, cut in triangles

Melt butter; stir in flour and cook until blended. Slowly add milk, stirring with whisk until mixture boils and thickens. Stir in cheeses and salt; remove from heat. Add a small amount of mixture to egg yolks, then add egg yolks to saucepan. Beat egg whites until stiff; fold a spoonful of whites into the mixture, then fold mixture into remaining egg whites. Grease a jellyroll pan and line with waxed paper. Leave an extra amount of waxed paper at each end, then grease and flour the waxed paper. Spread batter evenly on waxed paper. Bake 45 minutes or until surface springs back. Remove from oven and place another piece of waxed paper over soufflé. Invert. Remove baking pan and baked piece of waxed paper. Spread Spinach-Chicken Filling on soufflé. Roll lengthwise, using waxed paper to help roll. Grease baking sheet and slide roll onto pan. Overlap cheese triangles on top of roll and melt under broiler. Serve warm.

Spinach-Chicken Filling

½ cup	onions, chopped
¼ pound	mushrooms, chopped
2 tablespoons	butter, melted
2 (10 ounce) packages	frozen, chopped spinach

1 cup	cooked chicken, diced
1 (3 ounce) package	cream cheese
⅓ cup	sour cream
2 teaspoons	Dijon mustard
dash	nutmeg
	salt and pepper to taste

Sauté onion and mushrooms in butter. Stir in chicken, spinach, cream cheese and sour cream. Cook and stir until cheese melts. Add mustard, nutmeg, salt and pepper.

Connie Brink

Chicken
With Cucumbers

Serves: 6-8

8	chicken breasts
2 tablespoons	salad oil
1 clove	garlic, minced
1 pound	fresh mushrooms, sliced
4 tablespoons	flour
¼ cup	sherry
1½ cups	water
2 cubes	chicken-flavored bouillon
1½ teaspoons	salt
4	cucumbers
1 cup	sour cream

Brown chicken on all sides in hot oil with garlic; remove chicken. Sauté mushrooms with the garlic; remove mushrooms. Stir flour into garlic oil mixture. Gradually add sherry, water, bouillon cubes and salt. Cook until thickened. Add chicken, cover and simmer for 30 minutes. Peel cucumbers, quarter, scoop out seeds and pulp. Cut cucumbers into large chunks; add to chicken and cook 15-20 minutes or until chicken is tender and cucumbers are tender crisp. Stir in sour cream and mushrooms; heat but do not boil.

Lou Anderson

141

Skewered Chicken

Serves: 6-8

Entertaining is fun when serving this tender, delicate and delicious chicken. Garnish with cherry tomatoes and parsley.

3 whole	chicken breasts, split, skinned and boned
¼ cup	soy sauce
3 tablespoons	dry white wine
2 tablespoons	lemon juice
2 tablespoons	oil
¾ teaspoon	herb seasoning, crushed
1 clove	garlic, minced
½ teaspoon	ginger root, grated
¼ teaspoon	onion powder
dash	pepper

Cut chicken into strips 1¼ inches wide and ¼ inch thick. Thread strips loosely onto 6 to 8 skewers. Place skewers in 2 layers in a 12 x 7½ x 2 inch baking dish. Combine remaining ingredients. Pour over chicken. Cover. Chill 2-3 hours. Drain. Grill over hot coals 3-4 minutes per side.

Dixie Aftonomos

Apricot Glazed Chicken

Serves: 4

1	fryer, cut up
½ cup	apricot preserves
1 cup	apricot nectar
1 tablespoon	prepared mustard
1 tablespoon	soy sauce
1 tablespoon	lemon juice

Place chicken pieces in large, shallow baking dish. Combine apricot preserves, nectar, mustard, soy sauce and lemon juice and pour over chicken. Bake uncovered at 350 degrees F. for 1 hour or until tender. Occasionally baste chicken with sauce.

Linda Scoville

Chicken Divan

Serves: 4-6

This was served at Saint Simon's by the Sound Episcopal Church. Red apple rings were served with the green broccoli to provide a festive look during the Christmas season.

1 bunch	fresh broccoli
3 whole	chicken breasts, boned
1 (8 ounce) package	cream cheese, softened
⅓ cup	mayonnaise
⅛ teaspoon	curry powder
¼ teaspoon	sugar
3-4 tablespoons	cream or milk
	toasted almonds

Steam broccoli 5-8 minutes or until tender. Line a 9 x 13 x 2 inch casserole with broccoli. Steam chicken for 8 minutes and arrange on top of broccoli. Blend the cream cheese, mayonnaise, curry and sugar. Thin as necessary with cream. Pour cream mixture over the chicken. Bake in a preheated 350 degree F. oven for 20 minutes. Garnish with toasted almonds.

Nita Wilkinson

Golden Crust Pot Pie

Serves: 6

1	fryer, cooked and boned
1 cup	chicken broth
1 (10¾ ounce) can	cream of celery soup
1 cup	self-rising flour
½ cup	butter or margarine, melted
1 cup	milk

Place chicken in a buttered casserole. Mix broth and soup and pour over chicken. Mix flour, butter and milk and pour over the top. Bake at 350 degrees F. for 45 minutes to 1 hour. Peas, carrots and potatoes may be added for a very hearty, down-home treat.

Margaret Black

Chicken À La Lemone
Serves: 6

3 whole	large chicken breasts, boned
¼ cup	flour
½ teaspoon	salt
⅛ teaspoon	pepper
3 tablespoons	butter or margarine
1 cup	water
1 cube	chicken flavored bouillon
2 small	lemons

Pound chicken to ⅛ inch thickness with a wooden mallet. Mix flour, salt and pepper and use to coat chicken. Reserve remaining flour. In large skillet over medium heat, cook chicken in butter until lightly browned on all sides. Add more butter if necessary. Remove chicken. Reduce heat to low and pour reserved flour into pan drippings. Add water, bouillon cube and juice of half a lemon. Stir to loosen brown bits in skillet. Return chicken to skillet. Thinly slice remaining lemons and top chicken with lemon slices. Cover and simmer 5 minutes or until tender. Arrange chicken and lemon slices on a warm platter. Garnish with parsley or watercress.

Faye Dawson

Chicken Thyme
Serves: 4-5

A real time saver; a real taste pleaser!

¼ cup	margarine, melted
1 teaspoon	thyme
¼ cup	lemon juice
	salt and pepper to taste
	paprika to taste
1	fryer, cut up

Mix margarine, thyme, lemon juice, salt, pepper and paprika. Pour over chicken in a 9 x 13 x 2 inch pan. Let stand for 1 hour. Bake, covered, at 400 degrees F. for 40-60 minutes. Serve over rice.

Jan Bishop

Portuguese Chicken

Serves: 6

6 large	chicken breasts
	salt and pepper to taste
	paprika to taste
	garlic powder to taste
1 large	onion, chopped
1 large	green pepper, chopped
1/3 cup	catsup
1/3 cup	orange juice
2 tablespoons	soy sauce
1 teaspoon	dry mustard
1 tablespoon	flour
	orange slices

Place chicken in a casserole and sprinkle with salt, pepper, paprika and garlic powder. Top with onion and green pepper. Combine catsup, orange juice, soy sauce, dry mustard and flour. Pour over chicken. Bake at 350 degrees F. for 50 minutes. Add orange slices and cook 10 more minutes.

Ed Borkowski

Dijon Chicken Wellington

Serves: 4-6

6	chicken breasts, boned and skinned
	white wine
	chicken broth
1 (10 ounce) package	frozen puff pastry
12	ham pieces, cooked and thinly sliced
6 large	Swiss cheese slices
	Dijon mustard
	tarragon leaves

Poach chicken breasts in a mixture of equal parts wine and chicken broth. Cool. Roll out thawed puff pastry until thin. Wrap each chicken breast with 1-2 pieces of ham, then cheese, and spread with mustard. Sprinkle with tarragon. Wrap each chicken breast with puff pastry. Seal the edges. Bake at 350 degrees F. for 30-40 minutes.

Linda Sankey

Polynesian Chicken

Serves: 4-5

Peaches add a delightful touch to this South Sea Island dish.

	cooking oil
1 (3½ pound)	fryer, cut up
1 large	onion
1	green pepper
1 (29 ounce) can	sliced peaches, reserve syrup
1½ teaspoons	cornstarch
1 tablespoon	soy sauce
3 tablespoons	vinegar
2 medium	tomatoes, cut into sixths

Pour enough oil in skillet to cover ½ inch. Brown chicken on all sides and cook until tender. Peel onion, quarter and separate into layers. Cut green pepper into wide strips. Add onion and green pepper to chicken and cook until onion is transparent. Drain oil. Combine syrup from peaches, cornstarch, soy sauce and vinegar. Pour over chicken and cook until clear and slightly thick. Add peach slices and tomatoes. Heat 5 minutes. Serve over fluffy white rice.

Linda Scoville

South Sea Chicken

Serves: 4

1	fryer, cut into serving pieces
	salt and pepper to taste
½ cup	flour
4 tablespoons	butter
2	bay leaves
1 (4½ ounce) can	mushrooms, reserve liquid
2 tablespoons	lemon juice
2 tablespoons	Worcestershire sauce
½ cup	sherry or water

Season chicken with salt and pepper and dredge in flour. Place in a 9 x 13 x 2 inch casserole and dot with butter. Add bay leaves and mushrooms. Combine mushroom liquid, lemon juice, Worcestershire sauce and sherry. Pour over chicken. Cover and bake at 350 degrees F. for 1½ hours.

Sara Tras

Kiev With Mushroom Sauce

Serves: 4-8

An extra-special Kiev makes this a spendid way to dine!

4 whole	chicken breasts, skinned
	salt
1 tablespoon	green onion, chopped
1 tablespoon	parsley, chopped
¼ pound	butter, cut into 8 pieces
½ cup	flour
1 tablespoon	water
1	egg
½ cup	fine, dry bread crumbs
3 tablespoons	butter
½ pound	fresh mushrooms, sliced
1 tablespoon	flour
1 teaspoon	soy sauce
¾ cup	light cream

Cut each chicken breast in half lengthwise. Debone the chicken, being careful not to tear the meat. Place each piece of chicken between two pieces of clear plastic wrap. Working out from the center, pound with a wooden mallet to form cutlets not quite ¼ inch thick. Peel off wrap. Sprinkle with salt. Sprinkle onion and parsley over each cutlet. Place a piece of butter at the end of each cutlet. Roll meat as for a jellyroll, tucking in sides. Press ends to seal. Coat each roll with flour. Beat water with the egg. Dip rolls in the egg mixture, then roll in bread crumbs. Chill at least 1 hour. Fry chicken rolls in deep fat about 5 minutes or until golden brown. Set aside and keep warm. Melt remaining butter; add mushrooms and sprinkle with flour. Cook over medium heat, stirring occasionally, 8-10 minutes or until tender. Add soy sauce and slowly stir in cream. Cook and stir until mixture bubbles and thickens. Season to taste. Serve over chicken rolls.

Abigail Calhoun

147

Rolled Chicken Washington

Serves: 6-7

A gourmet's delight.

½ cup	fresh mushrooms, finely chopped
2 tablespoons	butter or margarine
2 tablespoons	flour
½ cup	light cream
¼ teaspoon	salt
dash	cayenne pepper
1 ¼ cups	sharp Cheddar cheese, grated
6-7	chicken breasts, boned and skinned
	salt
	flour
2	eggs, slightly beaten
¾ cup	fine, dry bread crumbs

Sauté mushrooms in butter for 5 minutes. Blend in flour and cream. Add salt and cayenne. Cook and stir until mixture becomes thick. Stir in cheese and cook over low heat, stirring constantly, until cheese is melted. Turn mixture into a pie plate. Cover. Chill thoroughly for about 1 hour. Cut the cheese mixture into 6 or 7 equal portions. Shape into short sticks. Place each chicken piece between two pieces of plastic wrap and pound with wooden mallet to form cutlets not quite ¼ inch thick. Peel away plastic wrap. Sprinkle with salt and place a cheese stick on each chicken piece. Tuck in sides and roll as for jellyroll. Seal edges. Dust chicken with flour, dip in egg and then in bread crumbs. Cover and chill thoroughly. An hour before serving, fry chicken rolls in deep, hot oil (375 degrees F.) for 5 minutes or until crisp and golden brown. Drain on paper towels. Place in a shallow baking dish and bake at 325 degrees F. for 30-45 minutes. Serve on a warm platter.

Mitzi Rowe

Capital
Chicken Casserole

Serves: 4

Add a green salad and chilled white wine for a very elegant and entertaining evening.

6 large	chicken breasts
2 tablespoons	oil
4 tablespoons	butter
½-1 pound	fresh mushrooms
2 tablespoons	flour
1 (10¾ ounce) can	cream of chicken soup
1 cup	sherry
1½ cups	chicken broth (canned)
½ cup	Half and Half
1 teaspoon	salt
¼ teaspoon	tarragon leaves
¼ teaspoon	pepper
1 (15 ounce) can	artichoke hearts
6	green scallions or green onions, chopped
2 tablespoons	parsley, chopped

Preheat oven to 350 degrees F. Brown chicken on all sides in oil and butter. Remove chicken and place in a long casserole. Sauté mushrooms in the oil and butter. Stir in flour. Add cream of chicken soup, sherry and broth. Simmer about 10 minutes or until thickened. Stir in Half and Half, salt, tarragon leaves and pepper. Pour sauce over the chicken. Bake uncovered for 1 hour. Add artichoke hearts, scallions and parsley. Bake 15 minutes more. Serve with wild rice.

Shelley Warner

Chicken Florentine

Serves: 8

8	chicken breasts, boned and skinned
	salt and pepper
1 (10 ounce) package	frozen, chopped spinach
1 cup	butter
1 (3 ounce) package	cream cheese, softened
½ teaspoon	lemon juice
½ cup	Swiss cheese, shredded
½ cup	Parmesan cheese, grated
	paprika

Pound chicken until thin; season with salt and pepper to taste. Cook and drain spinach. Melt ¼ cup butter and mix with spinach, cream cheese and lemon juice. In the middle of each chicken breast, spread 1 teaspoon butter, Swiss cheese and ¼ cup spinach mixture. Fold breast to cover stuffing. Spread 1 teaspoon butter on each chicken breast and sprinkle generously with Parmesan cheese and paprika. Place in a baking dish with a little water and dot with the remaining butter. Bake at 400 degrees F. for 30-45 minutes or until brown.

Martha Bayer

Curry Glazed Chicken

Serves: 4

An exotic and refined East Indies flavor to tempt any palate!

2 tablespoons	butter, melted
¼ cup	honey
2 teaspoons	curry powder
3 tablespoons	Dijon mustard
½ teaspoon	salt
1 (2-2½ pound)	fryer, cut into serving pieces

Preheat oven to 375 degrees F. Pour butter into a 9 x 13 x 2 inch metal baking pan. Stir in honey, curry powder, mustard and salt. Add chicken and turn to coat with honey mixture. Bake uncovered for 45 minutes. Turn and baste during baking. Serve over rice; in separate lotus bowls offer condiments of cashews, flaked coconut and pineapple.

Bettie Farr

Chicken Potato
Casserole

Serves: 6

⅓ cup	flour
	salt and pepper to taste
¼ teaspoon	paprika
1	fryer, cut into serving pieces
3 tablespoons	butter
3 large	potatoes, peeled and sliced
1 medium	onion, finely chopped
1 teaspoon	chicken bouillon
1 cup	hot water
1 (8 ounce) carton	sour cream

Combine flour, salt, pepper and paprika. Shake chicken in flour mixture to coat. Brown chicken on all sides in melted butter. Place potatoes on top of chicken in the skillet and sprinkle onion on top. Dissolve bouillon in hot water. Pour over chicken, potatoes and onion. Cover and cook on medium-low heat until chicken is tender. Remove potatoes and chicken. Stir sour cream into pan drippings. Heat until bubbly. Serve over the potatoes and chicken.

Winnis George

Miss Jewel's Chicken

Serves: 16

Great for entertaining large crowds. This may be prepared in advance, frozen, thawed and baked.

9 cups	water
3 packages	dry chicken noodle soup mix
2 cups	long grain white rice, uncooked
1 pound	sausage
1	green pepper, chopped
1 large	onion, chopped
1 cup	celery, chopped
	salt to taste
	curry powder to taste
2 (10¾ ounce) cans	cream of mushroom soup
10	chicken breasts, boned, skinned and cut into small pieces
½ cup	blanched almonds, toasted in melted butter

Bring water to a boil and add soup mix and rice; boil for 9 minutes, uncovered. Fry sausage in a large skillet; remove and drain. In the same skillet, sauté green pepper, onion and celery. Add vegetables and sausage to rice mixture. Season with salt and curry powder. Add cream of mushroom soup and chicken pieces. Mix well. Place mixture in 2 casserole pans and bake at 350 degrees F. for 45 minutes. Top with almonds and bake 15 additional minutes.

Jewel Howard

Chicken Enchiladas   *Serves: 6*

2 whole	chicken breasts
	salt to taste
1 cup	onion, chopped
1 clove	garlic, minced
2 tablespoons	butter or margarine
1 (16 ounce) can	tomatoes, sliced
1 (8 ounce) can	tomato sauce
¼ cup	green chilies, chopped
1 teaspoon	sugar
1 teaspoon	ground cumin
½ teaspoon	salt
½ teaspoon	oregano, crushed
½ teaspoon	basil, crushed
12	frozen tortillas, thawed
2½ cups	Monterey Jack cheese, grated
¾ cup	sour cream

Place chicken breasts in a saucepan and cover with water. Simmer 15-20 minutes or until tender. Drain, skin and debone chicken. Sprinkle with salt. Cut into 12 strips and set aside. In a saucepan, sauté onion and garlic in butter until tender. Add tomatoes, tomato sauce, chilies, sugar, cumin, salt, oregano and basil. Bring to a boil, reduce heat and simmer, covered, for 20 minutes. Remove from heat. Dip each tortilla in tomato mixture to soften. Place one piece of chicken and about 2 tablespoons of grated cheese on each tortilla; roll up and place seam-side down in a 13 x 9 x 2 inch baking dish. Blend sour cream into remaining sauce mixture and pour over tortillas. Sprinkle with remaining cheese. Cover and bake at 350 degrees F. for 40 minutes or until heated through.

Madelon David

Enchilada Verdes

Serves: 6

1 (3 pound)	fryer, boiled, save stock
1 large	onion, chopped
3 tablespoons	margarine
2 (10¾ ounce) cans	cream of chicken soup
2 teaspoons	chili powder
	salt and pepper to taste
5 cups	chicken stock
2 (4 ounce) cans	green chilies, chopped
2 packages	frozen flour tortillas
8 slices	American cheese
6 slices	Swiss cheese

Debone chicken and set aside. In a large skillet sauté onion in margarine and add chicken soup. Stir until well mixed. Add chili powder, salt, pepper and chicken stock. Cook slowly until well mixed. Add green chilies and cook for 30 minutes. Layer tortillas, chicken and American cheese in a large, rectangular pan. Pour the sauce over these layers. Cover with Swiss cheese. Bake at 350 degrees F. for 30 minutes. May be prepared in advance and refrigerated until ready to bake.

Nan Givhan

Chicken Waikiki

½ cup	flour
1 teaspoon	salt
¼ teaspoon	pepper
4	chicken breasts
⅓ cup	oil
1 (20 ounce) can	pineapple chunks, reserve syrup
1 cup	sugar
2 tablespoons	cornstarch
¾ cup	cider vinegar
1 tablespoon	soy sauce
¼ teaspoon	ginger
1 cube	chicken bouillon
1	green pepper, cut in rings

Season flour with salt and pepper. Coat chicken with this mixture and brown in oil. Place in shallow pan. Add enough water to reserved pineapple syrup to make 1¼ cups. In medium saucepan combine syrup, sugar, cornstarch, vinegar, soy sauce, ginger and bouillon cube. Bring to a boil and stir constantly for 2 minutes. Pour over chicken. Bake at 350 degrees F. uncovered for 30 minutes. Add pineapple chunks and green peppers. Bake 30 minutes longer.

Sandy Benton

Korean
Braised Chicken

Serves: 4

1 (3 pound)	chicken, skinned, boned and cubed
3 tablespoons	soy sauce
1 tablespoon	oil
2 small cloves	garlic, minced
⅛ teaspoon	cayenne pepper
1 tablespoon	cornstarch (optional)
½ cup	slivered almonds
1 teaspoon	butter or oil
1 cup	mushrooms, sliced
2	celery stalks, cut diagonally in 1 inch pieces
1 large	onion, cut into wedges and separate layers
¼ cup	green onion tops, sliced

Place chicken in a microwave-safe covered casserole. Mix soy sauce, oil, garlic, cayenne pepper and cornstarch. Pour over chicken and let marinate for at least 30 minutes. Place almonds and butter in a microwave-safe dish and microwave on HIGH for 4-5 minutes or until golden brown. Stir often. Add mushrooms, celery and onion wedges to the chicken. Cover and microwave on HIGH until chicken is opaque and tender or about 15 minutes. Stir often during cooking. Garnish with almonds and green onion tops. To make this authentically Korean, omit the cornstarch. However, most Americans prefer the thick sauce produced by the cornstarch.

Marilyn Chitwood

Island Chicken

Serves: 4

½ cup	celery, chopped
½ cup	onion, chopped
1 clove	garlic, chopped
2 tablespoons	oil
1 (15 ounce) can	tomato sauce with tomato bits
2 cups	cooked chicken, cubed
1 cup	cooked rice
1 teaspoon	curry powder
3 tablespoons	brown sugar
3 tablespoons	vinegar
1 ½ teaspoons	salt
1 fresh	pineapple

Sauté celery, onion and garlic in oil. When tender add all ingredients except pineapple. Simmer 25 minutes. Quarter and core whole fresh pineapple; do not remove leaves. Slash fruit. Mound chicken mixture on the pineapple sections. Cover with foil. Bake 30 minutes at 325 degrees F.

Lesley Blalock

Chicken Croquettes

Serves: 6-8

This may be prepared ahead of time and frozen. Thaw before frying or baking.

¼ cup	butter or margarine
3 tablespoons	flour
1 cup	milk
2 cups	cooked chicken, chopped
4 cups	fine bread crumbs
1 tablespoon	onion, chopped
1 tablespoon	parsley flakes
1	egg
	salt and pepper to taste

Combine butter, flour and milk. Boil and stir until thick and remove from heat. Set aside. Combine all other ingredients. Add to sauce mixture and mix well. Shape into 1 ½ inch balls. Deep fry or bake at 350 degrees F. for 20 minutes. Gravy may be made from the chicken stock and served warm over the croquettes.

Brenda Lloyd

157

Cornish Hens With
Wild Rice Stuffing

Serves: 2

¼ cup	celery, minced
¼ cup	shallots or onion, minced
2 tablespoons	green pepper, minced
2 tablespoons	butter or margarine
1⅓ cups	chicken broth
2 tablespoons	fresh parsley, minced
1 teaspoon	herb seasoning
⅔ cup	wild rice
2 (1-1¼ pound)	Cornish hens
	salt and pepper
¼ cup	butter or margarine
½ cup	red currant jelly
¼ cup	brandy

Sauté celery, shallots and green pepper in butter in a medium saucepan. Stir in next 3 ingredients, bring to a boil and add wild rice. Cover and reduce heat to medium-low and cook about 25 minutes. Remove giblets from hens and reserve for another use. Rinse hens with cold water and pat dry. Sprinkle cavities with salt and pepper. Stuff hens lightly with rice mixture. Close cavities and secure with wooden picks and truss. Place hens, breast-side up, in a shallow baking pan. Melt butter in a small saucepan. Brush hens with butter, reserving any remaining butter in saucepan. Bake hens at 375 degrees F. for 30 minutes. Combine jelly and brandy in saucepan with remaining butter. Cook over low heat, stirring often, until jelly melts. Brush hens with jelly mixture. Bake 30-40 additional minutes, depending on size of hens, basting every 10 minutes with jelly mixture.

Mitzi Rowe

Cornish Hens In Wine

Cornish hens
melted butter
salt
pepper
paprika
lemon juice
Worcestershire sauce
Tabasco sauce
thyme
garlic powder
consommé
white wine
fresh mushrooms, sliced

Baste each hen with a mixture of butter, salt, pepper, paprika, lemon juice, Worcestershire sauce, Tabasco sauce, thyme and garlic powder. Place hens in a roaster in about 1 inch of consommé and bake covered at 275 degrees for 2-2½ hours. When half done, add wine. About 30 minutes before removing from oven, add mushrooms. If more liquid is needed during baking, add more wine. Remove cover during the last 15 minutes of baking to brown.

Carolyn Pinkerton

Duck Casserole

Serves: 8

For a less expensive variation, use chicken. This casserole can be prepared in advance and frozen.

2	ducks
½ cup	onions, chopped
½ cup	butter
¼ cup	flour
1 (6 ounce) can	mushrooms
1 (5 ounce) package	brown and wild rice
1½ cups	Half and Half
1 tablespoon	parsley
1½ teaspoons	salt
¼ teaspoon	pepper
1 (4 ounce) package	sliced almonds

Cook duck in pressure cooker for 15 minutes. Retain ½ cup broth and dice meat to yield 3 cups. Sauté onion in butter. Stir in flour, ½ cup duck broth and mushrooms. Cook rice according to package directions. To the rice add the broth mixture, Half and Half, parsley, salt and pepper. Stir in duck. Pour into a 2 quart casserole. Sprinkle with almonds. Bake at 350 degrees F. for 25 minutes or until bubbly.

Susan Black

Seafood

Seafood

Grilled Mullet

Serves: 4

Mullet — an Okaloosa County tradition found at political gatherings, seafood festivals and the inspiration for the annual Boggy Bayou Mullet Festival. Mullet is served with cheese grits, cole slaw and hush puppies.

1½ pounds	mullet filets
	juice of 2-3 limes
½ cup	butter
1 teaspoon	salt
½ teaspoon	pepper

Place filets in a flat pan and squeeze lime juice on top. Refrigerate 4 hours to tenderize. When ready to cook, place on an oiled grill over hot coals and brush with butter. Season with salt and pepper. Baste frequently with butter as fish browns.

Lisa Madden

Fish Batter

Serves: 6

This can be used with shrimp!

3 pounds	fish filets
1 cup	buttermilk
1	lemon, sliced
	flour
2 cups	pancake mix
2½ cups	club soda
	oil

Cut filets in half to make triangles. Cover with buttermilk and lemon slices and refrigerate for 2 hours. Remove fish from buttermilk and discard lemon slices. Dredge fish in flour and let dry for a few minutes. Combine pancake mix and soda. Dip fish in batter and fry in hot, deep oil until golden brown.

Darlene Raim

Flounder With Crab Stuffing

Serves: 6

1 (3 pound) or 6 (¾ pound)	flounder, dressed
	Crabmeat Stuffing
¼ pound	butter, melted
¼ cup	lemon juice
2 teaspoons	salt
2 tablespoons	water
	paprika

Crabmeat Stuffing

½ cup	onion, chopped
⅓ cup	celery, chopped
⅓ cup	green pepper, chopped
2 cloves	garlic, finely chopped
⅓ cup	oil
2 cups	soft bread crumbs
3	eggs, beaten
1 tablespoon	parsley, chopped
2 teaspoons	salt
½ teaspoon	pepper
1 pound	crabmeat

Rinse flounder and pat dry. To prepare crabmeat stuffing, sauté onion, celery, green pepper and garlic in oil until tender. Add bread crumbs, eggs, parsley, salt, pepper and crabmeat. Mix thoroughly. Stuff fish loosely. Combine butter, lemon juice, salt and water. Place fish in a well-greased baking dish. Pour butter mixture over fish. Sprinkle with paprika. Bake at 350 degrees F. for 40-60 minutes.

Liz Cavanah

Fish Delish

Serves: 6

6 thick	fish filets (cobia, grouper, snapper or amberjack)
	salt and pepper to taste
½ cup	lemon juice
¼ cup	sherry
6 tablespoons	butter or margarine
½ cup	beef au jus or consommé
	parsley
	paprika
	Parmesan cheese, grated

Line a baking dish with foil using enough to fold and cover fish tightly. Place filets in dish and season with salt and pepper. Pour lemon juice and sherry over the fish. Put a tablespoon of butter on each filet. Pour in au jus or consommé. Cover tightly. Bake at 350 degrees F. for 1 hour or until fish is flaky. Open foil and sprinkle fish with parsley, paprika and Parmesan cheese. Broil until lightly browned and crisp on top. Spoon au jus over fish to serve.

Marsha Laughlin

Sesame Grilled Fish

Serves: 4

¼ cup	orange juice
2 tablespoons	catsup
2 tablespoons	soy sauce
1½ teaspoons	lemon juice
¼ teaspoon	pepper
2 teaspoons	sesame oil
1 tablespoon	brown sugar
1½ pounds	fish filets (amberjack, trigger fish, grouper)
1 tablespoon	sesame seeds, toasted

Combine orange juice, catsup, soy sauce, lemon juice, pepper, sesame oil and brown sugar. Mix well. Pour sauce over fish and marinate overnight. Grill fish over coals for 15 minutes or until fish flakes easily with a fork. Baste fish with marinade while grilling. Top with sesame seeds.

Bess Jones

Baked Stuffed Fish

Serves: 4

½ cup	celery, chopped
½ cup	green onion, chopped
1 clove	garlic, minced
½ cup	butter or margarine, divided
1 ½ cups	moist bread crumbs
½ pound	shrimp, boiled, peeled and chopped
½ pound	crabmeat
2 tablespoons	parsley, chopped
1	egg, slightly beaten
	salt, pepper and cayenne pepper to taste
4 medium	flounder or snapper

Sauté celery, onion and garlic in ¼ cup butter. Add bread crumbs, shrimp, crabmeat, parsley and egg; mix well. Season with salt, pepper and cayenne pepper. Split the thick side of fish to form a pocket for stuffing. Brush with melted butter. Salt, pepper and stuff cavity. Melt remaining butter in a shallow baking dish and place fish in dish. Cover and bake at 375 degrees F. for 25 minutes or until fish flakes easily. Remove cover and bake 5 minutes more.

Shirley Grace

Barbecued Amberjack

Serves: 4-6

Great for outdoor entertaining; grouper or mackerel can be used.

½ cup	butter, melted
½ teaspoon	garlic powder
1 tablespoon	Worcestershire sauce
1 teaspoon	lemon pepper
	juice of 1 lemon
3 pounds	amberjack, cut into 8 ounce filets

Combine butter, garlic powder, Worcestershire sauce, lemon pepper, and lemon juice. Place fish on the grill over hot coals. Baste with sauce and cook until fish is flaky or about 20 minutes.

Debi Roberts

Flounder Rolls Florentine

Serves: 6

Add a little white wine or sour cream to the soup mixture to vary this recipe.

2 tablespoons	onion, chopped
2 tablespoons	butter or margarine, melted
1 (10 ounce) package	frozen chopped spinach, thawed
½ cup	Swiss cheese, shredded
1 teaspoon	salt
¼ teaspoon	Tabasco sauce, divided
6	flounder filets
1 (10¾ ounce) can	cream of mushroom soup

Sauté onion in butter until tender. Add spinach; cover and cook 5 minutes. Remove from heat; add cheese, salt and ⅛ teaspoon Tabasco; mix well. Place ⅓ cup spinach filling in the center of each fish filet and roll as for jellyroll, securing with wooden picks. Place on a greased 2 quart baking pan. Mix soup with the remaining ⅛ teaspoon Tabasco sauce and pour over the fish. Bake at 375 degrees F. for 25-35 minutes or until fish flakes when tested with a fork. Garnish with lemon slices.

Sylvia Gash

Hearts And Sole

Serves: 2

1 tablespoon	butter
1 pound	sole or flounder filets
⅔ cup	white wine
⅓ cup	water
1	shallot, chopped
½ teaspoon	salt
¼ teaspoon	white pepper
¼ pound	fresh mushrooms, sliced
1 (15 ounce) can	artichoke hearts
1	egg yolk
1 cup	cream

Melt butter in skillet; add fish, wine and water. Add shallots, salt, pepper, mushrooms and artichoke hearts. Cover and simmer for 10-12 minutes. Remove fish and artichoke hearts and transfer to a shallow baking pan to keep warm. Cook sauce over high heat for 3-4 minutes to reduce liquid slightly. Stir often. Mix egg yolk and cream. Stir a small amount of the hot sauce into the egg mixture. Then add the egg mixture to the sauce. Cook over low heat, stirring constantly until smooth. Pour over the fish and broil until the top is golden brown.

Grouper Parmesan

Serves: 2-4

1 cup	sour cream
¼ cup	Parmesan cheese
1 tablespoon	grated onion
1 tablespoon	lemon juice
dash	tabasco
	paprika
½ cup	Parmesan cheese
	Grouper

Mix the above ingredients. Cut fish into squares, omitting bones. Cover with mixed ingredients. Sprinkle with Parmesan cheese and paprika. Bake at 350 degrees F. for 35 minutes.

Easy! Quick! Triggerfish or scamp may be substituted.

Linda and Malcolm Patterson

Grouper Kiev

Serves: 6

¼ pound	butter, softened
2 tablespoons	parsley, chopped
1 tablespoon	lemon juice
¾ teaspoon	Worcestershire sauce
¼ teaspoon	Tabasco sauce
1 clove	garlic, finely chopped
½ teaspoon	salt
dash	pepper
2 pounds	grouper filets
2 tablespoons	water
2	eggs, beaten
½ cup	flour
3 cups	bread crumbs
	oil

Combine butter, parsley, lemon juice, Worcestershire sauce, Tabasco sauce, garlic, salt and pepper. Place butter on a piece of waxed paper and form into a roll. Chill until firm. Cut filets into 6 portions. With a sharp knife, cut horizontally along one side of each portion to form a pocket. Cut the cold, seasoned butter into 6 pieces. Place a piece of butter into each pocket and secure the opening with a wooden pick. Mix water and eggs. Roll fish in flour, dip into eggs and roll in bread crumbs. Chill for 1 hour. Fry in deep fat heated to 375 degrees F. for 2-3 minutes or until color is golden brown and fish flakes easily when tested with a fork. Drain on paper towel. Remove pick to serve.

Liz Cavanah

Gulf Coast
Mackerel Bake
Serves: 6

2 pounds	mackerel steaks
1 teaspoon	salt
¼ teaspoon	pepper
¼ cup	flour
	oil
1 ½ cups	fresh tomatoes, peeled, seeded and diced
1 cup	fresh mushrooms, sliced
¼ cup	dry vermouth
¼ teaspoon	garlic, crushed
½ cup	soft bread crumbs
2 tablespoons	butter, melted

Rinse and dry fish. Sprinkle both sides with salt and pepper. Roll in flour. Place fish in a single layer in a 12 inch skillet and fry for 2-3 minutes on both sides in hot oil. Turn fish carefully. Place in a single layer in a well-greased shallow baking dish. Combine tomatoes, mushrooms, vermouth and garlic in a saucepan. Bring to a boil, stirring constantly. Pour hot sauce over the fish. Mix bread crumbs with melted butter and sprinkle over the top. Bake at 375 degrees F. for 20-25 minutes.

Liz Cavanah

Snapper With
Sour Cream Stuffing

Serves: 6

3-4 pounds	fresh snapper, cut into filets
1½ teaspoons	salt
2 tablespoons	margarine, melted, or oil

Cut a pocket in each filet in order to stuff. Sprinkle fish inside and out with salt. Stuff fish loosely with Sour Cream Stuffing. Close opening with skewers or wooden picks. Place fish on a greased baking pan. Brush with margarine or oil. Bake at 350 degrees F. for 40-60 minutes, or until fish flakes easily. Baste while cooking.

Sour Cream Stuffing

¾ cup	celery, chopped
½ cup	onion, chopped
¼ cup	margarine, melted
4 cups	dry bread cubes
½ cup	sour cream
¼ cup	lemon, peeled and diced
2 tablespoons	lemon rind
1 teaspoon	paprika
1 teaspoon	salt

Sauté celery and onion in margarine. Combine all ingredients and mix thoroughly.

Donna Bridgford

Stuff-It

3	green onions, chopped
1 medium	white onion, chopped
3	celery stalks, chopped
½ cup	butter or margarine, melted
1 pound	crabmeat
½ cup	seasoned bread crumbs
½ teaspoon	paprika
	salt and pepper to taste
2 tablespoons	lemon juice
1 pound	shrimp, peeled, cooked and chopped
1	egg

Sauté green onions, white onions and celery in butter. Add crabmeat, stirring constantly. Add bread crumbs, paprika, salt, pepper and lemon juice. Stir. Add shrimp and beaten egg. The egg holds the mixture together. If too loose, add more bread crumbs. Never cover the mixture. This can be served in individual ramekins garnished with a lemon wedge or as an entrée used as stuffing for shrimp or fish. Freeze in patties and thaw when needed.

TO STUFF FISH: Use filets and mound on top or stuff dressed fish such as flounder, snapper or grouper. To stuff a whole fish, have the fish slit down the middle to form a pocket; sprinkle with lemon juice and salt and Stuff-It. Garnish with lemon slices and paprika. Add water or wine to baking dish so fish will not stick to bottom. Cook uncovered at 400 degrees F. until fish flakes when fork tested.

TO STUFF SHRIMP: Peel and devein large shrimp, leaving tails intact. Slit backs for stuffing and Stuff-It. Place in baking pan and add wine or water. Cook at 400 degrees F. until done or about 10-15 minutes.

Bill Burris

Shrimp And Crabmeat Casserole

Serves: 6

Wonderful as an appetizer or a main course served with Sherried Cheesé Grits and a fresh spinach salad.

2 large	eggs
⅔ cup	milk
⅓ cup	sherry
¼ teaspoon	salt
½ teaspoon	pepper
dash	Tabasco sauce
3½ cups	Cornflakes, crushed
8 tablespoons	butter or margarine
½ cup	celery, finely diced
½ cup	green onion, chopped
¼ cup	green pepper, diced
1 pound	crabmeat
1 pound	shrimp, cooked, peeled, deveined and chopped
dash	paprika
¼ cup	lemon juice

Beat eggs and milk together. Add sherry, salt, pepper and Tabasco sauce; mix well. Pour mixture over 3 cups of crushed Cornflakes and let stand while preparing the vegetables. Melt 4 tablespoons of butter in a heavy skillet and add celery, onion and green pepper. Cook slowly until soft. Pour vegetables over Cornflake mixture and mix well. Add crabmeat and shrimp.

Place 2 tablespoons of butter, cut into small pieces, in the bottom of a shallow baking dish. Spoon the crabmeat and shrimp mixture into the baking dish. Mix the remaining Cornflakes with remaining butter and paprika. Sprinkle Cornflake mixture and lemon juice evenly over casserole. Bake at 350 degrees F. for 30-45 minutes, or until casserole is slightly browned and all liquid has been absorbed.

Edna Knight

Royal Seafood Casserole

Serves: 8-10

This can be prepared in advance and frozen.

2 (10½ ounce) cans	cream of shrimp soup
½ cup	mayonnaise
1 cup	onion, chopped
¾ cup	milk
½ teaspoon	seasoned salt
½ teaspoon	salt
⅛-¼ teaspoon	red pepper
⅛-¼ teaspoon	nutmeg
⅛-¼ teaspoon	cayenne pepper
2 pounds	shrimp, cooked and cleaned
2 pounds	scallops, sautéed and drained
1 (5 ounce) can	water chestnuts, drained and sliced
1½ cups	celery, diced
3 tablespoons	parsley
2 cups	raw rice, cooked and drained
	paprika
	slivered almonds, sautéed

Blend soup, mayonnaise, onion and milk. Add seasoned salt, salt, red pepper, nutmeg and cayenne pepper and mix well. Add shrimp, scallops, water chestnuts, celery, parsley and rice. Add more milk at this point if casserole is too dry. Pour mixture into a shallow, buttered casserole dish. Top with almonds and paprika. Bake at 350 degrees F. for 30-40 minutes or until hot and bubbly.

Jean Bowman

Captain's Casserole

Serves: 8

Can be prepared in advance and frozen. Thaw before baking.

2 large	onions, chopped
1 large	green pepper, chopped
1 (8 ounce) can	mushrooms, stems and pieces, drained
1 clove	garlic, minced
4 tablespoons	bacon drippings
6 slices	dry toast, crumbled
2 (10¾ ounce) cans	chicken broth
1 tablespoon	Worcestershire sauce
1 teaspoon	salt
½ teaspoon	pepper
½ teaspoon	celery salt
1 teaspoon	oregano
2 dashes	Tabasco sauce
¾ cup	parsley, chopped
1 pound	white lump crabmeat
¾ cup	cracker crumbs
3 tablespoons	butter
	paprika

Sauté onion, green pepper, mushrooms and garlic in bacon drippings. Soak toast in 1 can chicken broth and add to the vegetables. Add Worcestershire sauce, salt, pepper, celery salt, oregano and Tabasco sauce. Simmer in skillet until blended. Add parsley and remaining chicken broth to moisten casserole. Add crabmeat, blend thoroughly and turn into a buttered casserole. Cover with cracker crumbs, dot with butter and sprinkle with paprika. Bake at 350 degrees F. for 20 minutes.

Mitzi Rowe

Crabmeat Ponchartrain   *Serves: 6*

1 pound	lump crabmeat
6 strips	bacon, cooked crisp
1 teaspoon	dry mustard
½ teaspoon	paprika
½ teaspoon	celery salt
½ teaspoon	Tabasco sauce
½ cup	chili sauce
1 teaspoon	tarragon vinegar
1½ cups	mayonnaise

Divide crabmeat into 6 portions and place in 6 ramekins. Heat in the oven and top with bacon strips. Blend together mustard, paprika, celery salt and Tabasco sauce. Add remaining ingredients. Cover warm crabmeat with the sauce and glaze under the broiler.

Louise Burris

Crabtrap Bake   *Serves: 4*

Looks attractive for lunch or dinner served in scallop baking shells or au gratin dishes.

1 large	onion, chopped
¾ cup	celery, chopped
1	green pepper, chopped
½ cup	butter
1 pound	crabmeat
1½ teaspoons	prepared mustard
1 cup	seasoned bread crumbs
2 tablespoons	mayonnaise
1 (10¾ ounce) can	cream of mushroom soup
2	eggs, beaten

Sauté onion, celery and green pepper in butter. Add the remaining ingredients and mix well. Fill baking shells or a 2 quart casserole and bake at 350 degrees F. for 20-30 minutes.

Lynne Handsel

Creamy Crab Bake

Serves: 4

This can be prepared in advance and frozen.

4 tablespoons	butter, melted
2 tablespoons	flour
1 ½ cups	Half and Half or milk
½ teaspoon	salt
1 tablespoon	lemon juice
1 tablespoon	Worcestershire sauce
1 ½ teaspoons	creamed-style horseradish
1 teaspoon	dry mustard
2 teaspoons	parsley
½ pound	lump crabmeat
	buttered bread crumbs

Blend butter and flour in a saucepan over low heat. Slowly add Half and Half and cook; stir until sauce thickens. Add salt, lemon juice, Worcestershire sauce, horseradish, mustard and parsley. Pour sauce over the crabmeat and blend well. Be careful not to separate the lumps. Pour the mixture into shells or in au gratin dishes and top with bread crumbs. Bake at 350 degrees F. for 30 minutes.

Elizabeth Street

Sunny Seafood

Serves: 4-6

1 (5 ounce) package	yellow rice
2 cups	margarine
1	green pepper, chopped
1	onion, chopped
1 rib	celery, sliced
1 (10 ounce) can	rotel tomatoes (drained)
1 (10¾ ounce) can	cream of mushroom soup
2 pounds	shrimp, peeled
1 pound	crabmeat
1 bunch	green onion tops, chopped

Cook rice according to package directions. Sauté green pepper, onion and celery in margarine. Add tomatoes and mushroom soup. Add shrimp and cook until shrimp turn pink. Combine vegetables with rice; add crabmeat and onion tops and mix well. Place in a 9 x 13 x 2 inch casserole and bake at 350 degrees F. for 30-40 minutes.

Mardel Pogue

Stewed Crabs

A good meal to serve outdoors. Messy to eat, but worth it!

1½ cups	water
½ cup	margarine
1 medium	onion, chopped
	salt and pepper to taste
1 dozen	crabs, cleaned
1½ tablespoons	cornstarch
½ cup	water

Simmer water, margarine and onion until onions are clear. Add salt, pepper and crabs; simmer for 10 minutes. Remove crabs and thicken sauce with cornstarch that has been dissolved in the water. Return crabs to the sauce and heat. Serve crabs and sauce with warm, buttered French bread.

Polly McCall

Lou's Shrimp Sauce

1 cup	butter
1 tablespoon	Worcestershire sauce
2 tablespoons	soy sauce
1 tablespoon	tarragon vinegar
1 teaspoon	salt
7-8 dashes	Tabasco sauce
	juice of 2 large lemons

Place all ingredients in a saucepan. Heat but do not boil. Serve sauce in individual bowls for each guest. Serve with boiled shrimp.

Lesley Blalock

Shrimp Remoulade

²/₃ cup	salad oil
¼ cup	cider vinegar
3 heaping tablespoons	Creole mustard
3 teaspoons	horseradish
1 teaspoon	Worcestershire sauce
1 teaspoon	salt
½ teaspoon	red pepper
½ cup	celery, finely chopped
¼ cup	green onion, finely chopped
2 tablespoons	catsup
1 clove	garlic, finely minced
2 pounds	shrimp, cooked, peeled and deveined

Mix all ingredients thoroughly except shrimp. Add shrimp and let marinate in the sauce 6-12 hours or overnight. Serve on shredded lettuce or with crackers.

Jacque Hale

Shrimp And
Asparagus Stir-Fry

Serves: 2-3

¼ cup	sesame seeds
1 tablespoon	butter or margarine
1	onion, finely sliced
2 tablespoons	soy sauce
1 pound	shrimp, peeled and deveined
	fresh asparagus

Heat sesame seeds in a 9 inch skillet until toasted. Set aside. Sauté onion in butter until clear. Add soy sauce, shrimp and asparagus and stir-fry until shrimp is pink and the asparagus is tender crisp. Place on a serving platter and sprinkle with sesame seeds.

Lois Walsh

Shrimp Stroganoff

Serves: 4

Serve with Tomato Rockefeller or Summertime Tomatoes.

¼ cup	onion, minced
5 tablespoons	butter
1 ½ pounds	raw shrimp, peeled
½ pound	fresh mushrooms, sliced
1 tablespoon	flour
1 ½ cups	sour cream (room temperature)
1 ¼ teaspoons	salt
	pepper to taste
	cooked yellow rice
	artichoke hearts, quartered

In a large skillet sauté onion in 4 tablespoons melted butter until soft. Add shrimp and sauté 3-5 minutes or until pink and just cooked. Transfer shrimp and onion to a heated serving dish and keep warm. In the same skillet sauté mushrooms in remaining butter over medium-high heat until browned. Sprinkle with flour and cook for 2 minutes, stirring constantly. Reduce heat and stir in shrimp and onion, sour cream, salt and pepper. Cook, stirring for 2-3 minutes or until shrimp are heated. Do not boil, and be careful not to curdle the sour cream. Serve over yellow rice tossed with artichoke hearts.

Jeanne Burford

Shrimp Veronique

Serves: 4

1 medium	onion, chopped
4 tablespoons	margarine
1 (10¾ ounce) can	cream of mushroom soup
1 tablespoon	curry powder
1 tablespoon	lemon juice
	salt and pepper to taste
3 pounds	shrimp, peeled and deveined
1 (16 ounce) can	white seedless grapes
4 tablespoons	sour cream
	rice, cooked and drained

Sauté onion in margarine until clear; add cream of mushroom soup and stir until blended. Add curry powder, lemon juice, salt, pepper and shrimp. Cook for 8-10 minutes. Add grapes and stir in sour cream. Cook until mixture begins to bubble. Serve over rice.

Frances Frakes

Shrimp Jambalaya

Serves: 4-6

Crabmeat can be added to this. Scallops may be used instead of the shrimp.

2 medium	onions, chopped
1 small	green pepper, diced
½ clove	garlic, diced
¼ cup	lean salt pork, diced
4 tablespoons	butter
1 tablespoon	Worcestershire sauce
3 (8 ounce) cans	tomato sauce
2-3 pounds	shrimp, peeled
3 cups	water
2 cups	rice

Sauté onions, green pepper, garlic and pork in butter. Add Worcestershire sauce, tomato sauce, shrimp and water. Cover and simmer for 30 minutes. Add rice and cook until tender or about 30 minutes more. Add more water if sauce becomes too thick. Stir often. Serve immediately.

Captain Royal Melvin

Shrimp Creole   *Serves: 4-6*

4 tablespoons	bacon drippings
2 tablespoons	flour
1 large	onion, chopped
1 cup	celery, chopped
1 clove	garlic, finely chopped
1 (28 ounce) can	tomatoes
1 (8 ounce) can	tomato sauce
1 teaspoon	salt
⅛ teaspoon	pepper
1 teaspoon	parsley
dash	oregano
2	bay leaves
1 ½ pounds	shrimp, shelled and deveined
	cooked rice

Brown flour in bacon drippings. Add onions, celery and garlic and cook until onions are clear. Add tomatoes, tomato sauce, salt, pepper, parsley, oregano and bay leaves. Cook until all ingredients are well-done and sauce is thick. Add shrimp and simmer for 15 minutes. Remove bay leaves and serve over hot rice.

Sylvia Gash

Spiced Shrimp   *Serves: 6-8*

1 ½ cloves	garlic, crushed
2 ½ teaspoons	chili powder
1 ½ cups	oil
1 tablespoon	ground turmeric
1 tablespoon	basil
2 tablespoons	vinegar
1 teaspoon	salt
	pepper, freshly ground
3 pounds	shrimp, peeled and deveined

Mix all ingredients and pour over shrimp. Marinate for at least 6 hours. Pour shrimp and marinade into a shallow pan and broil for 6-10 minutes, turning once.

Sally Simpson

Broiled Shrimp   *Serves: 2-3*

1-1 ½ pounds	shrimp, peeled and deveined
¼ cup	butter or margarine, melted
1 ½ teaspoons	lemon juice
½ teaspoon	Worcestershire sauce
¼ teaspoon	Tabasco sauce

Arrange shrimp in a broiler pan. Combine remaining ingredients. Pour over shrimp. Broil until shrimp are pink and butter mixture golden.

Jenny Brand

Bay Bounty Oysters

Serves: 6

1 pint	oysters, reserve liquid
¼ cup	celery, minced
2 tablespoons	onion, minced
½ cup	butter, melted
1 teaspoon	garlic juice
⅛ teaspoon	pepper
1 teaspoon	salt
¾ cup	milk
1 teaspoon	lemon juice
1 tablespoon	parsley, chopped
2 cups	cracker crumbs
½ cup	Cheddar cheese, grated

Sauté oysters in liquid until the edges begin to curl; drain. Sauté celery and onion in butter. Combine oysters, celery and onion with all remaining ingredients except ½ cup cracker crumbs and cheese. Turn into a greased 1½ quart casserole. Combine remaining cracker crumbs and cheese and sprinkle over the top. Bake at 350 degrees F. for 30 minutes or until light brown and bubbling.

Lou Baughman

Bewlay Maney's Scalloped Oysters

Serves: 8-10

1 (12 ounce) package	oyster crackers
1 pint	oysters
½ cup	butter or margarine
	salt and pepper to taste
2 cups	milk

Grease a 9 x 13 x 2 inch casserole. Crush ⅓ of the oyster crackers and place in the bottom of the casserole. Top with ⅓ of the oysters and dot with butter, salt and pepper. Repeat layers two more times, ending with crushed oyster crackers on top. Pour in milk. Bake at 350 degrees F. for 1 hour.

Caroline Maney

Oysters Rockefeller   *Serves: 4-6*

2 (10 ounce) packages	frozen chopped spinach
2½ bunches	parsley
1 bunch	green onions
4 tablespoons	butter
1 teaspoon	anise or anise seed
5 tablespoons	Worcestershire sauce
5 tablespoons	lemon juice
1 teaspoon	salt
1½ teaspoons	pepper
8 dashes	Tabasco sauce
1 tablespoon	vinegar
4 squeezes	anchovy paste (approximately 1½ teaspoons)
1 tablespoon	Drambuie (optional)
1 pint	oysters
	raw bacon pieces
	Parmesan cheese, grated

Cook spinach according to package directions. Use a food processor or meat grinder to finely chop the parsley, onion and spinach. Melt butter and add anise, Worcestershire sauce, lemon juice, salt, pepper, tabasco sauce, vinegar, anchovy paste and Drambuie. Mix with spinach mixture. Place oysters in shells or ramekins and cover with sauce. Top with small pieces of bacon and Parmesan cheese. Bake at 400 degrees F. for 15 minutes. Garnish with lemon slices, if desired.

Wilson Bellenger

Oysters 'N
Artichoke Hearts

Serves: 8-10

½ cup	butter
1 large	white onion, finely chopped
3	green onions, chopped
3 cloves	garlic, crushed
1 (14 ounce) can	artichoke hearts, quartered
1 (6 ounce) jar	marinated artichoke hearts, cut up
2 (10 ounce) cartons	oysters, reserve liquid
1 (10¾ ounce) can	cream of mushroom soup
¼ cup	dried parsley
1 tablespoon	Worcestershire sauce
1 teaspoon	poultry seasoning
½ teaspoon	salt
	pepper to taste
¼ cup	sherry
1 (4 ounce) can	mushrooms, chopped
1 tablespoon	pimento
1 cup	Italian bread crumbs
2 (10 ounce) packages	frozen patty shells

Sauté onion, green onion and garlic in butter until tender. Add artichoke hearts and cook for 10 minutes. Strain oysters and chop. Add oysters and about half the liquid to the vegetables. Add soup, parsley, Worcestershire sauce, poultry seasoning, salt, pepper, sherry and mushrooms. Simmer for 15 minutes. Add pimento and bread crumbs, mixing well. Pour into a greased 1½ quart baking dish and bake at 350 degrees F. until hot and bubbly. Bake pastry shells as directed on the package. Fill shells with oyster mixture until overflowing.

Suzanne Seemann

Oyster Spaghetti

Serves: 6

6-8 dozen	oysters, reserve liquid
1 clove	garlic, minced
1 bunch	green onions, chopped
1 cup	parsley, chopped
¼ cup	olive oil
1 cup	mushrooms, sliced
½ teaspoon	basil
1 pound	spaghetti, cooked and drained
½ cup	Parmesan cheese, grated
	salt and pepper to taste

Drain oysters well, reserving liquid. Sauté garlic, onions and parsley in olive oil. Add mushrooms and oysters. Cook over low heat until oysters curl. Add basil. Toss oyster mixture with spaghetti, Parmesan cheese, salt and pepper. If spaghetti is too dry, add some oyster liquid.

Carola Lipsey Bacque

Salmon Loaf

Serves: 4-6

Vary this recipe by adding chopped green pepper and celery.

2½ cups	red salmon, flaked
1 cup	tomatoes
½ teaspoon	salt
¼ teaspoon	paprika
	pepper
1 tablespoon	onion, chopped
¾ cup	cracker crumbs
3 tablespoons	butter, melted
3	eggs, separated

Skin salmon, remove bones. Mix all ingredients except eggs. Add well-beaten egg yolks and fold in stiffly-beaten egg whites. Place in a greased loaf pan. Start baking in a cold oven at 325 degrees F. for 1¼ hours.

Alice Calhoun

187

Scallops Veronique

Serves: 4

¼ cup	green onion, chopped
3 tablespoons	butter or margarine
1 pound	fresh scallops
1 teaspoon	cornstarch
2 tablespoons	dry sherry
⅓ cup	mayonnaise
1 (2½ ounce) jar	sliced mushrooms, drained
½ cup	seedless green grapes, halved
½ teaspoon	salt
dash	pepper
2 tablespoons	fine, dry bread crumbs

Sauté green onion in butter in a large skillet over medium heat until tender. Add scallops, cover and simmer 5 minutes. Combine cornstarch and sherry until smooth; add to scallops. Stir gently until mixture reaches a boil; cook 1 minute or until slightly thickened. Add mayonnaise, mushrooms, grapes, salt and pepper. Spoon scallop mixture into 4 individual baking shells or cups. Sprinkle with bread crumbs. Broil 5 inches from heat for 2 minutes or until lightly browned.

Gail Bailey

Tangy Tartare Sauce

Yield: 1½ cups

Easy and delicious. Serve with broiled, smoked or fried fish.

1 cup	mayonnaise
2 teaspoons	onion, grated
1 teaspoon	dry mustard
2 tablespoons	parsley, minced
1 clove	garlic, crushed
2 tablespoons	dill pickle, minced
2 tablespoons	capers
1 tablespoon	green onion, minced

Combine all ingredients and refrigerate at least 1 hour before serving.

Suzanne Seemann

Vegetables

Vegetables

Artichoke-Mushroom Velvet

Serves: 4-6

An excellent accompaniment to turkey or other poultry dishes and takes less than 15 minutes to prepare.

3 (14 ounce) cans	artichoke hearts
1 (6 ounce) can	mushrooms, sliced and drained
1 envelope	chicken gravy mix
⅛ teaspoon	crushed thyme
⅛ teaspoon	crushed marjoram
1 cup	Swiss cheese, grated
2 tablespoons	dry white wine
1 cup	bread crumbs, buttered

Combine artichoke hearts and mushrooms and place in a 1-quart casserole dish. Prepare chicken gravy mix according to package directions. Remove mixture from heat; add thyme, marjoram and cheese. Stir until cheese melts; add wine and pour over artichoke and mushroom combination. Top with bread crumbs. Bake uncovered at 350 degrees F. for 25-30 minutes.

The Fort Walton Beach Woman's Club

Crusty Asparagus

Serves: 4

This dish is easily doubled for party fare.

2 (15 ounce) cans	asparagus, drained, reserve liquid
2 cups	light cream
6 tablespoons	butter
6 tablespoons	flour
¾ teaspoon	salt
⅛ teaspoon	white pepper
2 cups	sharp Cheddar cheese, grated
1 cup	poultry stuffing mix

Preheat oven to 400 degrees F. Add enough cream to asparagus liquid to measure 3 cups. Melt 4 tablespoons butter and blend in flour. Add asparagus liquid and cream mixture; heat and stir until thickened. Add salt, pepper and 1 cup of cheese. Cook and stir until cheese is melted. Arrange asparagus in a buttered 2 quart casserole and top with cheese sauce. Toss remaining cheese with stuffing mix; sprinkle over top and dot with remaining butter. Bake uncovered 10-12 minutes or until bubbly and light brown.

Carol Daniel

Broccoli With
Lemon Sauce

Serves: 6-8

½ cup	slivered almonds
1 tablespoon	butter
2 (10 ounce) packages	frozen broccoli spears
2 (3 ounce) packages	cream cheese
⅓ cup	milk
1 tablespoon	lemon peel, grated
½ teaspoon	ground ginger
¼ teaspoon	salt

Combine almonds and butter in a small bowl and microwave on HIGH for 3 minutes or until light brown. Set aside. Place broccoli in a 2 quart dish, cover, and microwave on HIGH for 4-5 minutes. Uncover and continue to cook for 6-7 minutes or until crisp. Set aside covered. Place cream cheese in a 2 cup glass measure and microwave at LOW for 6 minutes; stir until smooth. Add remaining ingredients and stir. Microwave on HIGH for 3-4 minutes or until hot. Place broccoli on a serving platter and pour sauce over the top. Sprinkle with almonds to serve.

Jo Ann Mosblech

193

Broccoli Puff

Serves: 6

Reminiscent of a vegetable soufflé!

2 (10 ounce) packages	frozen cut broccoli
1 (10¾ ounce) can	cream of mushroom soup
½ cup	sharp American cheese, shredded
¼ cup	milk
¼ cup	mayonnaise
1	egg, beaten
¼ cup	fine, dry bread crumbs
1 tablespoon	butter, melted

Cook broccoli according to package directions, omitting salt. Drain thoroughly. Place broccoli in a 10 x 6 x 1 ½ inch baking dish. Stir together soup and cheese. Gradually add milk, mayonnaise and egg; stir until blended. Pour over broccoli; combine bread crumbs and butter and sprinkle over top. Bake at 350 degrees F. for 45 minutes or until lightly browned.

Susan Johnson

Marinated Brussels Sprouts

Serves: 6

1 ½ pounds	fresh Brussels sprouts or 2 (10 ounce) packages frozen Brussels sprouts
⅓ to ½ cup	tarragon vinegar
½ cup	salad oil
1 small clove	garlic, minced
1 tablespoon	sugar
1 teaspoon	salt
2 tablespoons	green onion, thinly sliced
dash	hot pepper sauce

Cook Brussels sprouts in 1 inch of boiling, salted water for 8-10 minutes or until tender. Drain well. Combine remaining ingredients and toss with Brussels sprouts. Chill at least 8 hours. Drain and serve.

Mitzi Rowe

Sicilian Broccoli

Serves: 4-6

1 bunch	fresh broccoli
2 tablespoons	butter, melted
1 tablespoon	green onion, chopped
2 cloves	garlic, minced
1½ tablespoons	flour
1 cup	chicken stock
4	anchovies, finely chopped (optional)
½ cup	black olives, sliced
	pepper
2 cups	Mozzarella cheese, shredded

Cook broccoli in salted water until tender. Drain and set aside on serving dish. In a small saucepan, sauté onions and garlic in butter. Sprinkle with flour and add chicken stock. Stir until thickened. Simmer 5 minutes, stirring constantly. Add anchovies, olives, pepper and cheese. Stir until cheese melts and pour over broccoli.

Mary Starnes King

Cabbage Key Casserole

Serves: 6

1 head	cabbage, cut into pieces
2 tablespoons	butter
¼ teaspoon	salt
1 cup	milk
2 tablespoons	flour
2 teaspoons	pepper
½ cup	Velveeta cheese
1 cup	buttered cracker crumbs

Cook cabbage in water until almost tender. Drain and place in casserole dish. Combine other ingredients in a saucepan and cook until smooth. Pour sauce over cabbage; top with buttered cracker crumbs and bake at 400 degrees F. for 20 minutes.

Margie DeBolt

Baked
Swiss Cauliflower
Serves: 6

1 large head	cauliflower
½ cup	bread crumbs
2¾ cups	Swiss cheese, shredded
1½ cups	Half and Half
3	egg yolks, beaten
¼ teaspoon	ground nutmeg
½ teaspoon	salt
¼ teaspoon	pepper
¼ cup	butter, melted

Wash cauliflower and break into flowerets. Cook, covered, for 10 minutes in a small amount of boiling, salted water. Drain. Place cauliflower in a buttered 1½ quart shallow baking dish. Combine remaining ingredients except butter. Pour over cauliflower and drizzle butter over top. Bake at 350 degrees F. for 15-20 minutes.

Mitzi Rowe

Tangy
Mustard Cauliflower
Serves: 6

Elegant microwave magic!

1 medium head	cauliflower
2 tablespoons	water
½ cup	mayonnaise
1 tablespoon	green onion, chopped
1 teaspoon	prepared mustard
½ cup	Cheddar cheese, grated

Place washed cauliflower in a 1½-2 quart casserole. Add water, cover, and microwave on HIGH for 8-9 minutes. Combine mayonnaise, onion and mustard and spread over the cauliflower. Sprinkle with cheese. Microwave on HIGH for 1½-2 minutes to melt cheese.

Carol Burda

Choctaw Corn Pudding

Serves: 6-8

6 ears	fresh corn or 2 (12 ounce) cans whole kernel corn, drained
6 tablespoons	butter, melted
2 tablespoons	sugar
2 tablespoons	flour
½ cup	light cream
4	eggs, well beaten
1½ teaspoons	baking powder
2 tablespoons	butter, melted
2 tablespoons	brown sugar
¼ teaspoon	cinnamon

Cut kernels from corn; set aside. Combine butter and sugar and heat in a small saucepan. Stir in flour and remove from heat. Gradually stir in cream; add eggs and baking powder. Mix well. Stir mixture into corn and pour into a 1½ quart buttered casserole. Bake at 350 degrees F. for approximately 40 minutes or until knife inserted in center comes out clean. Drizzle butter over the top and sprinkle with a mixture of brown sugar and cinnamon. Return to the oven and bake 5-7 more minutes.

Sally Simpson

Tipsy Carrots

Serves: 4

1 (16 ounce) bag	fresh carrots, thinly sliced
	water
2 tablespoons	butter, melted
¼ cup	orange liqueur
	salt

Cook carrots in a small amount of water for a few minutes. Add butter, liqueur and salt to taste. Simmer for 30 minutes, covered.

Gail Ferguson

197

Eggplant Parmesan

Serves: 4-6

For a variation, mix a combination of ¼ cup onion, green pepper and celery and sprinkle on eggplant layers.

1 medium	eggplant, sliced ¼-½ inch thick
2	eggs, beaten
	Italian seasoned bread crumbs
¾ cup	oil
1 (15 ounce) can	tomato sauce with tomato bits, onions, celery and green pepper
1 (8 ounce) can	tomato sauce
1 (8 ounce) package	shredded Mozzarella cheese
1 cup	Parmesan cheese, grated

Dip eggplant slices into egg and cover with bread crumbs. Brown in hot oil and drain. In an 8 x 8 inch casserole layer half of the eggplant, tomato sauces and cheeses; repeat layers, topping with cheese. Bake at 350 degrees F. for 30 minutes. Let sit 5 minutes before serving.

Dinah Remington

Creole Onions

Serves: 6-8

4-5 medium	onions, peeled and sliced
2 slices	bacon, chopped
1 clove	garlic, minced
¼ cup	green pepper, chopped
1 cup	ham, chopped
1 (8 ounce) can	tomato sauce
	salt and pepper to taste
½-1 cup	Cheddar cheese, shredded

Boil onions 10-12 minutes or until tender. Fry bacon. Add garlic and green pepper; sauté until tender. Add ham and tomato sauce; stir and simmer for 5 minutes. Place onions in a greased 2 quart casserole dish. Pour sauce over the onions, add salt and pepper and bake at 325 degrees F. for 25 minutes. Remove and add cheese; return to oven to melt.

Suzanne Seemann

Onion Pie

Serves: 6-8

1 cup	Ritz crackers, finely crumbled
¼ cup	butter, melted
2 cups	Vidalia onions or yellow onions, thinly sliced
2 tablespoons	butter
2	eggs
¾ cup	milk
¾ teaspoon	salt
dash	pepper
¼ cup	sharp Cheddar cheese, grated
	paprika
	parsley

Mix cracker crumbs with butter. Press into an 8-inch pie plate. Sauté onions in 2 tablespoons butter until clear. Spoon into crust. Beat eggs with milk, salt and pepper; pour over onions. Sprinkle with cheese and paprika. Bake at 350 degrees F. for 30 minutes or until a knife inserted in the center comes out clean. Sprinkle with parsley before serving.

Lou Baughman

Potato Delight

Serves: 4-6

5 medium	potatoes
½ cup	butter, melted
6	green onions, chopped
2 cups	sour cream
2 cups	sharp Cheddar cheese, grated
2 (10¾ ounce) cans	cream of chicken soup
1 cup	potato chips, crushed

Cook potatoes with skins. Let cool. Peel and grate. Sauté onions in butter. Combine sour cream, one half of the cheese and soup. Pour over the potatoes in a 2 quart casserole. Sprinkle remaining cheese and crushed potato chips over the top. Bake at 300 degrees F. for 30 minutes.

Mrs. Pat Hunt

Potatoes Roquefort

Serves: 6

6 medium	baking potatoes
¼ cup	oil
½ cup	Roquefort cheese, firmly packed
¼ cup	heavy cream
1 teaspoon	salt
¼ teaspoon	pepper
⅓ cup	bread crumbs, toasted
¼ clove	garlic, pressed
3 tablespoons	butter, melted

Scrub potatoes and rub skins with oil. Bake at 400 degrees F. for 1-1¼ hours or until done. Allow to cool. Slice skin from top of each potato and scoop out pulp, leaving shells intact. Mash pulp and add cheese. Beat with electric mixer until blended. Gradually add cream. Stir in salt and pepper. Stuff shells with potato mix. Combine bread crumbs, garlic and butter. Sprinkle over potatoes and bake at 350 degrees F. for 20-25 minutes.

Jo Ann Mosblech

Crab-Stuffed Potato

Serves: 4-6

3 large	Idaho baking potatoes
¼ cup	butter
¼-½ cup	milk
4 teaspoons	onion, finely chopped
1 teaspoon	salt
1 cup	Cheddar cheese, grated
1 cup	crabmeat, cooked
	paprika

Bake potatoes until done. Split in half lengthwise and scoop out pulp. Reserve shells. Mash potato pulp with butter, milk, onion and salt until mixture is smooth and creamy. Stir in grated cheese and crabmeat. Fill shells with mixture. Sprinkle with paprika. Bake at 450 degrees F. for 15 minutes.

Stuffed Yams
Serves: 6

6 medium	sweet potatoes or yams
¼ cup	butter or margarine, softened
1 tablespoon	brown sugar
1 teaspoon	salt
dash	pepper
	hot milk
¼ cup	walnuts, finely chopped

Scrub potatoes with a brush. Bake at 425 degrees F. for 40-60 minutes or until done. Cut a lengthwise slice from top of each. Scoop out pulp, being careful not to break the shell. Mash the potatoes and add butter, brown sugar, salt, pepper and enough hot milk to moisten. Beat with electric mixer until fluffy. Fold in nuts. Pile mixture lightly into the potato shells. Garnish with a walnut half if desired. Bake at 350 degrees F. for 15-20 minutes.

Mitzi Rowe

Wild Rice Party Dish
Serves: 4

Beautiful served around roast on a meat platter.

½ cup	butter or margarine
1 (6 ounce) box	long grain and wild rice mix
½ cup	slivered almonds
2 tablespoons	green onion, chopped
½ pound	fresh mushrooms, sliced
2 tablespoons	sherry
3 cups	chicken broth

Place all ingredients except broth in a heavy skillet. Cook until rice is well coated, stirring frequently. Combine with chicken broth and place in a casserole. Cover and refrigerate or freeze. When ready to serve, return to room temperature; bake, covered, at 325 degrees F. for 1¼ hours, or until liquid is absorbed.

Martha Bayer

Calcutta Rice

Serves: 6

Good with lamb, duck or chicken.

2 tablespoons	butter or margarine
1-2 teaspoons	curry powder
1 teaspoon	seasoned pepper
1 cup	celery, diced
2 medium	apples, peeled, cored and sliced
¼ cup	sliced almonds
3 cups	rice, cooked

Melt butter and stir in curry powder and pepper. Add celery, apples and almonds. Sauté until tender crisp. Stir in rice and heat thoroughly.

Jo Ann Mosblech

Caribbean Casserole

Serves: 8

Excellent side dish with beef!

¼ cup	butter, melted
1 cup	onion, chopped
4 cups	rice, cooked and warm
2 cups	sour cream
1 cup	cottage cheese
1 large	bay leaf, crumbled
½ teaspoon	salt
⅛ teaspoon	pepper
3 (4 ounce) cans	green chilies, drained
2 cups	sharp Cheddar cheese, grated
	parsley, chopped

Preheat oven to 350 degrees F. In a large skillet, sauté onion in butter until golden. Remove from heat. Stir in warm rice, sour cream, cottage cheese, bay leaf, salt and pepper. Toss to mix. Cut the chilies in half lengthwise and remove seeds. Layer rice, chilies and cheese in a 2 quart baking dish. Bake for 25 minutes. Sprinkle with parsley to garnish.

Adrienne Parker

Spinach And Artichoke Casserole
Serves: 12-16

Recipe may be halved. Freezes well.

4 (10 ounce) packages	frozen chopped spinach
10 tablespoons	butter, divided
8 tablespoons	flour
2 cups	milk
1	onion, chopped
1 teaspoon	celery salt
1 teaspoon	garlic salt
1 teaspoon	salt
¾ (6 ounce) roll	Jalapeño cheese
2 (14 ounce) cans	artichoke hearts, drained and quartered
1 cup	raw brown rice, cooked
1 cup	herb-seasoned stuffing mix
2 (8 ounce) cans	mushrooms, sliced
	bread crumbs, buttered

Cook spinach according to package directions. Drain well and reserve 1 cup spinach liquid. Melt 8 tablespoons butter in a saucepan. Add flour, stirring until blended. Add spinach liquid and milk slowly, stirring to avoid lumps. Cook until thick and smooth. Sauté onion in remaining 2 tablespoons butter until tender. Add onion to sauce mixture. Add seasonings and cheese and stir until cheese melts. Add artichoke hearts, brown rice, stuffing and mushrooms. Combine sauce with spinach. Serve immediately or place in a 3-quart casserole and top with bread crumbs; bake at 350 degrees F. until bubbling.

Louise Burris

Posh Squash

Serves: 6-8

3 tablespoons	butter
½ cup	cracker crumbs
½ cup	pecans, chopped
¼ cup	water
½ teaspoon	salt
1 ½ pounds	yellow squash, sliced
¼ cup	mayonnaise
1	egg, beaten
1 cup	Cheddar cheese, shredded
2 tablespoons	butter, melted
1 ½ teaspoons	sugar
½ teaspoon	instant onion

Place butter in a 1 quart casserole and microwave on HIGH ½ minute to melt. Add cracker crumbs and pecans, microwave on HIGH 1 minute. Stir, and continue to microwave on HIGH 1 more minute. Pour mixture onto waxed paper and set aside. In the same dish, place water, salt and squash; cover and microwave on HIGH 4 minutes. Stir and continue to microwave 4-6 additional minutes. Drain well. Combine final 6 ingredients; pour over squash. Mix well and microwave on MEDIUM for 4 minutes. Stir, add crumb topping and microwave on MEDIUM 2-4 minutes or until center is set. Let stand 5 minutes before serving.

Gwen Hansen

Seaside Stuffed Squash

Serves: 6

An attractive way to serve squash — and good.

1 pound	summer squash
½ cup	green pepper, chopped
½ cup	Cheddar cheese, grated
½ cup	sour cream
½ cup	onion, minced
4 slices	bacon, cooked and crumbled

Boil squash 10-12 minutes. Slice lengthwise. Scoop out pulp. Add remaining ingredients to pulp and mix well. Fill squash with mixture, placing each in a baking dish. Bake 20 minutes in a 350 degrees F. preheated oven. May be prepared ahead of time and refrigerated until ready to bake.

Marni Roake

Squash Okaloosa

Serves: 6

3 cups	zucchini, grated
2 cups	carrots, grated
1	onion, grated
½ (8 ounce) package	herb-seasoned stuffing mix
⅓ cup	butter, melted
1 cup	cream of chicken soup
½ cup	sour cream

In a skillet, lightly cook the zucchini, carrots and onion to reduce water. In a bowl, combine stuffing with melted butter. Combine half the stuffing, soup, sour cream and cooked vegetables. Place mixture in a 2 quart buttered casserole dish and sprinkle with the remaining stuffing. Bake at 350 degrees F. for 25-30 minutes.

Gloria Roberts

Tomatoes Rockefeller

Serves: 12

12 thick slices	tomato
2 (10 ounce) packages	frozen creamed spinach
1 cup	seasoned bread crumbs
1 cup	plain bread crumbs
6	green onions, chopped
6	eggs, slightly beaten
¾ cup	margarine, melted
¼ cup	Parmesan cheese, grated
¼ teaspoon	Worcestershire sauce
¼ teaspoon	garlic, minced
1 teaspoon	salt
½ teaspoon	black pepper
1 teaspoon	thyme (optional)
1 teaspoon	Accent
¼ teaspoon	Tabasco sauce

Cook spinach according to package directions. Add remaining ingredients except tomatoes. Arrange tomatoes in a single layer in a buttered baking dish. Mound spinach mixture on top of tomato slices. Bake at 350 degrees F. for 15 minutes.

Ann Brown

Indian Vegetables

Serves: 4

2 tablespoons	oil
2	onions, chopped
½ pound	cauliflower, cut into flowerets
½ pound	broccoli, chopped
	salt to taste
	curry powder to taste
½ cup	roasted peanuts
¼ cup	raisins
	sour cream

Heat a skillet. Add oil, onions, cauliflower, broccoli, salt and curry powder. Sauté until vegetables are tender. Add peanuts and raisins. Remove to serving dish and add a dollop of sour cream to each serving.

Debi Roberts

Desserts

Desserts

Banana's Grand Marnier   *Serves: 6-8*

Fancy dessert to serve at table using flambé pan and heating element.

4 tablespoons	sugar
3 tablespoons	butter
¼ cup	orange juice
1 ounce	Grand Marnier or Curacao
4-8	bananas
1 jigger	cognac
1 pint	vanilla ice cream

In flambé pan, heat sugar until it melts and is a clear light brown. Stir in butter, orange juice and Grand Marnier (or Curacao). Cook for 8-10 minutes over low heat. Slice bananas lengthwise and add to sauce. Cook 3 minutes. Pour cognac over bananas and ignite. Serve over ice cream.

Martha Kilpatrick

Pineapple Cream Loaf

May substitute bananas or add bananas with the pineapple.

½ cup	margarine
1½ cups	powdered sugar
2	egg yolks
½ teaspoon	lemon extract
1 (8 ounce) can	crushed pineapple, drained
1 (8 ounce) carton	sour cream
2	egg whites, stiffly beaten
8	lady fingers, split

Cream margarine with sugar until fluffy. Add yolks 1 at a time, beating well after each. Stir in lemon extract and pineapple. Fold in sour cream and egg whites. Line the bottom of a loaf pan with split lady fingers. Top with pineapple mixture. Alternate layers ending with pineapple mixture. Chill 6-8 hours.

Jewel Howard

209

English Trifle

Pour ½ cup sherry over cake pieces before pouring strawberries over trifle for an added flavor.

1 package	yellow cake mix
1 (16 ounce) package	strawberry halves
2 cups	vanilla pudding, ready to serve
1 cup	whipping cream, chilled
¼ cup	sugar
¼ cup	toasted slivered almonds
8 whole	strawberries

Bake cake mix in oblong, 13 x 9 x 2-inch pan, as directed on package. Cut cake crosswise in half. (Freeze one half for future use.) Cut other half into 8 pieces; split each piece horizontally. Arrange half the pieces in a 2-quart glass serving bowl, cutting pieces to fit. Pour half the strawberries over cake; spread with half the pudding. Repeat. Cover; chill at least 8 hours. In a chilled, stainless bowl, beat cream and sugar until stiff; spread over trifle. Sprinkle with almonds; garnish with whole strawberries. To serve, spoon trifle into dessert dishes.

Virginia Glynn Barr

Sensational Strawberries

¾ cup	sugar
½ cup	heavy cream
¼ cup	light corn syrup
2 tablespoons	butter
½ cup	Heath Toffee candy bars, chopped
1 quart	fresh strawberries, washed and hulled
	sour cream

Combine sugar, cream, corn syrup and butter in a saucepan. Bring to a boil and cook for 3 minutes. Stir occasionally. Remove from heat and add candy. Stir until most of the candy is dissolved. Cool. Serve strawberries topped with a dollop of sour cream and drizzle with sauce.

Ellen Deckert

Peaches With Amaretto Sabayon

Serves: 4

4 whole	peaches, peeled
	Amaretto liqueur

Remove pit from peaches leaving peach whole. This can be done by slicing a small hole off the stem end and using a demi-tasse spoon to loosen pit from peach flesh. Sprinkle inside with liqueur and chill.

Sabayon Sauce

8	egg yolks
⅔ cup	sugar
1½ cups	Amaretto liqueur (may use Grand Marnier)
2 cups	heavy cream
	almonds, slivered

In top of double boiler, combine all ingredients except almonds and cream. Whip over simmering water until sauce is thick. Remove and cool mixture. Whip cream and fold into Amaretto mixture; then spoon all of mixture into and over peaches. Garnish with almonds. Serve immediately.

Virginia Glynn Barr

Crunchy Peanut Butter
Ice Cream
Serves: 8

4	eggs, beaten
1½ cups	sugar
2 (14 ounce) cans	sweetened condensed milk
8 ounces	crunchy peanut butter
1 teaspoon	vanilla
	whole milk

Combine all ingredients except whole milk. Mix well. Pour into a 4 quart ice cream freezer can. Fill the can to the full line with whole milk. Freeze as usual. Remove dasher from can, being careful not to get ice or salt into the ice cream. Replace lid. Cover freezer with newspaper and/or cloth and allow to ripen for at least 1 hour.

Liz Cavanah

Keith's Piña Colada
Ice Cream
Serves: 8-10

This ice cream is yummy!

4	eggs, beaten
3 cups	sugar
1 (13 ounce) can	evaporated milk
3 pints	Half and Half
1 tablespoon	vanilla
1 (8 ounce) can	crushed pineapple, drained
1 (8½ ounce) can	cream of coconut
1 cup	flaked coconut

Mix all ingredients; pour into a 4 quart ice cream freezer and freeze.

Keith Amiel

Almond Torte

Serves: 6-8

1 ½ cups	flour, not sifted
1 ½ cups	sugar
pinch	salt
2	eggs
1 cup	butter, melted
2 tablespoons	almond extract
	slivered almonds

Mix by hand all dry ingredients (except for almonds). Add eggs and stir well. Pour in melted butter and extract. Mix well by hand. Pour into greased quiche dish. Sprinkle almonds on top. Bake at 350 degrees F. for 30-40 minutes or until golden on top. Serve with ice cream or whipped cream and sprinkle with almond liqueur.

Joe Kemp

French Silk Cream

Serves: 4-5

Serve in parfait or sherbet glasses, or chocolate cups topped with whipped cream, for a very rich and elegant dessert.

½ cup + 2 tablespoons	butter, softened
1 cup	sugar
2 (1 ounce) squares	unsweetened chocolate, melted
1 ½ teaspoons	vanilla extract
¼ teaspoon	almond extract
3	eggs

Cream butter and sugar, mixing until light and fluffy. Add chocolate and vanilla. Add eggs 1 at a time and beat at medium speed for 5 minutes after each egg is added. After mixture is beaten, chill for at least 2 hours before serving.

Virginia Glynn Barr

Pizza Fruit Platter
Yield: 2 pizzas

1 package	yellow cake mix, divided
¼ cup	water
2	eggs
¼ cup	butter or margarine
¼ cup	brown sugar, packed
½ cup	nuts, chopped
2 (2 ounce) envelopes	dessert topping mix
2 pints	strawberries
2 (20 ounce) cans	pineapple chunks
4 dozen	seedless green grapes
2	bananas, peeled and sliced

Combine half of the dry cake mix, water, eggs, butter and brown sugar in mixing bowl; mix thoroughly. Blend in remaining cake mix. Fold in nuts. Divide batter evenly in two. Preheat oven to 350 degrees F. Line bottoms of two 12 inch round pizza pans with aluminum foil. The batter will be sticky, but spread it to the edges of the pans. Bake for 15-20 minutes. Cool and remove the cake from the pan. You will have to peel the foil off the bottom and then turn the cake onto a large, round serving dish.

Prepare topping mix as directed on packages and spread over the cakes. Halve the strawberries, leaving 14 whole, 7 for the center of each cake. Arrange fruit in a circular pattern over topping. Start with halved strawberries on outer edge, then arrange pineapple chunks, grapes, banana slices and end with whole strawberries in center. Drizzle apricot glaze over fruit. Refrigerate until serving time. Cut into pie-shaped wedges.

Apricot Glaze

1 cup	apricot preserves
4 tablespoons	water

Heat apricot preserves with water until melted. Remove from heat. Strain and cool.

Louise Burris

Coconut Cake

Serves: 16

2 cups	sugar
2 cups	self-rising flour
2 teaspoons	baking powder
¼ teaspoon	salt
5	eggs
1 cup	oil
½ cup	milk
1 teaspoon	vanilla
1 teaspoon	coconut flavoring
1 (3½ ounce) can	coconut

Glaze

1 cup	sugar
½ cup	water
4 tablespoons	margarine
1 teaspoon	coconut flavoring

Combine sugar, flour, baking powder and salt. Add the remaining ingredients and mix well. Pour into a greased and floured Bundt pan. Bake at 350 degrees F. for 1 hour. Combine all ingredients for glaze and cook 1 minute over high heat. Remove hot cake from pan. Pour half of the glaze into the cake pan. Place cake back into the pan and pour rest of glaze over the top. Cover and let soak several hours.

Sandy Benton

Apple Dapple Cake

Serves: 10

This is a moist cake. Good for luncheons, snacking, or a summer dessert.

1¾ cups	sugar
3	eggs
¾ cup	oil
¼ teaspoon	salt
2 cups	flour
1 teaspoon	cinnamon
1 teaspoon	vanilla
1 teaspoon	baking soda
1 cup	nuts
4 cups	fresh apples, peeled and chopped
⅓ to ¾ cup	raisins, scalded

Mix in order given; pour into a greased and floured 13x9x2-inch pan. Bake at 350 degrees F. for 45 to 50 minutes.

Jean Blumer

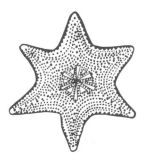

Hershey Bar Cake

Serves: 10

This cake is so moist, rich, and delicious that it needs no glaze or icing.

9 ounces	Hershey chocolate bars
1 (16 ounce) can	Hershey chocolate syrup
1 cup	butter or margarine
2 cups	sugar
4	eggs
2½ cups	flour
1 cup	buttermilk
½ teaspoon	soda
2 teaspoons	vanilla
1 cup	chopped nuts

Melt chocolate bars and half of the syrup over hot water. Cream butter with sugar. Add eggs 1 at a time, beating after each addition. Add chocolate mixture and the rest of the chocolate syrup. Add flour, buttermilk mixed with soda, vanilla and nuts. Beat well. Bake in a large, greased and papered tube pan in a 300 degree F. oven for 1½ hours.

Helen Schulz

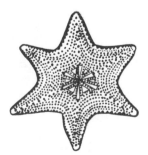

Mississippi Mud Cake   *Serves: 10-12*

1 cup	butter or margarine
½ cup	cocoa
2 cups	sugar
4	eggs, slightly beaten
1½ cups	flour
pinch	salt
1½ cups	nuts, chopped
1 teaspoon	vanilla
	miniature marshmallows
	Chocolate Frosting

Melt butter and cocoa together. Remove from heat and stir in sugar and eggs; mix well. Add flour, salt, nuts and vanilla; mix well. Spoon batter into a greased 13 x 9 x 2 inch pan and bake at 350 degrees F. for 35-45 minutes. Sprinkle marshmallows on top of the warm cake; cover with Chocolate Frosting.

Chocolate Frosting

1 (16 ounce) box	powdered sugar
½ cup	milk
⅓ cup	cocoa
4 tablespoons	butter or margarine, softened

Combine all ingredients and mix until smooth. Frosting will harden as it cools.

Sally Simpson

Oatmeal Cake

This is excellent as a dessert or in the morning for brunch.

1¼ cups	boiling water
1¼ cups	oatmeal
½ cup	oil
1¼ cups	flour
1 teaspoon	soda
2 teaspoons	baking powder
1 teaspoon	cinnamon
1 teaspoon	salt
2	eggs, whole
2	egg whites
1 cup	brown sugar
1 cup	granulated sugar
1 teaspoon	vanilla

Pour boiling water over oatmeal and mix well. Add oil. In separate bowl, sift dry ingredients together. Add to oatmeal mixture. Add eggs and remaining ingredients. Bake at 350 degrees F. in a greased and floured 13 x 9 x 2 inch pan for 30-35 minutes. Remove from oven and, while still hot, spread with topping.

Topping

½ cup	butter or margarine, melted
1 cup	brown sugar
1 (3½ ounce) can	coconut
½ cup	pecans, coarsely chopped
2	egg yolks
½ teaspoon	vanilla

Combine all ingredients and spread over hot cake. Place cake back in oven under broiler for just a few seconds until "lightly browned."

Betty Sahm

Pineapple Cheesecake

Serves: 10

Rich, light — super!

2 cups	graham cracker crumbs
1½ tablespoons	sugar
3 tablespoons	butter, melted
3 (8 ounce) packages	cream cheese, softened
1 cup	sugar
4	eggs
1 (8¼ ounce) can	crushed pineapple, drain, reserve syrup
1 tablespoon	lemon juice
1 teaspoon	lemon rind, grated
¼ cup	sugar
1½ cups	sour cream
½ teaspoon	vanilla

Combine graham cracker crumbs, 1½ tablespoons sugar and butter. Mix well. Press into the bottom and halfway up the sides of a 10-inch springform pan. Beat cream cheese until light and fluffy. Gradually add sugar, beating well. Add eggs one at a time, beating well after each. Stir pineapple, lemon juice and lemon rind into cheese mixture and spoon into crust. Bake at 325 degrees for 1 hour and 15 minutes. Cool thoroughly.

Combine ½ cup reserved pineapple juice and ¼ cup sugar. Cook over medium heat until sugar dissolves and mixture begins to thicken. Cool thoroughly. Stir in sour cream and vanilla. Spread over top of cheesecake and chill well.

Sandy Benton

Susan's Carrot And Pecan Cake

Serves: 15

1½ cups	salad oil
2 cups	sugar
2 cups	flour
2 teaspoons	baking powder
1 teaspoon	baking soda
1 teaspoon	cinnamon
1 teaspoon	salt
4	eggs
3 cups, packed	carrots, finely chopped
1 cup	pecans, chopped

Combine oil and sugar; mix well. Sift together dry ingredients. Sift half of dry ingredients into sugar mixture. Sift in remaining dry ingredients alternately with eggs, one at a time. Add carrots and mix well. Add pecans. Bake in three 0 inch greased pans at 325 degrees F. for 25 minutes or until done. Spread frosting over cake. Best if stands, well-covered, overnight in refrigerator.

Frosting

10 tablespoons	butter, softened
1 (8 ounce) package	cream cheese, softened
1 (3 ounce) package	cream cheese, softened
1 (16 ounce) box	powdered sugar
1 teaspoon	vanilla
1 cup	pecans, finely chopped

Combine butter, cheese, sugar and vanilla. Add nuts and spread over cake.

Susan Lee

Chocolate Chip Cupcakes

Yield: 12-14 cupcakes

FILLING

½ cup	sugar
1 (8 ounce) package	cream cheese, softened
pinch	salt
1	egg
1 cup	chocolate chips

Cream together sugar and cream cheese. Add salt and egg, mixing well. Stir in chocolate chips.

BATTER

1½ cups	flour
1 cup	sugar
1 teaspoon	soda
¼ teaspoon	salt
¼ cup	cocoa
1 cup	water
½ cup	vegetable oil
1 teaspoon	vinegar
1 teaspoon	vanilla
	paper cupcake cups
	chopped pecans
	sugar

Combine all dry ingredients. Stir in liquid ingredients and beat until smooth. Fill muffin tins, lined with paper cups, half full. Add a heaping teaspoon of filling into the center of each cup. Sprinkle with sugar and pecans. Bake at 350 degrees F. for 25-30 minutes.

Pam Williams

Cake Mix Cookies

½ cup	cooking oil
2	eggs
1 box	cake mix, chocolate

Mix all ingredients — can add chocolate chips or nuts (1 cup). Drop by teaspoonfuls onto ungreased cookie sheet. Bake at 350 degrees F for 10 minutes.

Linda Carr

Italian Wedding Cookies   *Yield: 8 dozen*

These are beautiful at weddings done in the wedding colors or at Christmas done in red and green. This is an old family recipe that originated in northern Italy.

6	eggs
½ cup	shortening
¼ cup	oil
1 cup	sugar
dash	salt
4 teaspoons	anise flavoring or
	2 teaspoons anise oil
1 teaspoon	baking powder for every
	cup of flour
5-6 cups	flour (preferably 5½ cups)
	powdered sugar

Beat eggs and add the remaining ingredients. Knead until dough can be handled easily. Roll into 1 inch balls. Bake at 350 degrees F. until lightly browned or for 10-15 minutes. Let cool. Dip in colored or white powdered sugar of medium consistency. Freezes well.

Elizabeth Bennett

Walnut Delights   *Yield: 3 dozen*

	1 cup	brown sugar, firmly packed
	½ cup	butter, softened
	1 teaspoon	vanilla
	1	egg
	1¾ cup	flour
	½	baking soda
	¼	salt
Topping	1 cup	chopped walnuts
	½ cup	brown sugar, firmly packed
	¼ cup	dairy sour cream

In a large bowl, cream sugar and butter until light and fluffy. Blend in vanilla and egg. Gradually add flour, soda and salt to creamed mixture, mixing well. Shape dough into 1-inch balls; place 2 inches apart on ungreased cookie sheet. With thumb, make imprint in center of each cookie. Combine topping ingredients; fill each cookie with 1 teaspoon topping. Bake at 350 degrees F. for 10-14 minutes or until delicately browned.

Sugar Mill Sweets

Sugar Beach
Sugar Cookies
Yield: 6 dozen

This recipe is dedicated to Adam Carr, who suggested our cookbook title.

1 cup	butter
2 cups	sugar
3	eggs
1 teaspoon	vanilla
1 teaspoon	almond extract
4 cups	flour, sifted
2 teaspoons	baking powder

Cream butter and sugar; add eggs and beat until fluffy. Add vanilla, almond, flour and baking powder. Refrigerate until dough is firm. Roll about ¼ of dough out at a time on a floured board to ⅛ inch thickness. Cut out cookies with cookie cutter and bake on cookie sheet at 325 degrees F. for 10 minutes or until light brown. Sprinkle with colored or SUGAR BEACH WHITE sugar.

Refrigerator
Nut Cookies
Yield: 5-6 dozen

Keep these in your freezer for a quick snack or dessert.

1 cup	butter, softened
1 cup	sugar
1 cup	light brown sugar
2	eggs
3½ cups	flour
½ teaspoon	soda
1 cup	nuts, chopped

Cream butter and sugars. Add eggs and beat until fluffy. Add flour and soda; mix well. Fold in nuts. Roll mixture on waxed paper to form logs. Freeze. When ready to bake, cut frozen logs into wafer-thin slices. Place on a cookie sheet and bake at 350 degrees F. for 5 minutes.

Bobbie Sibbet

Black Bottom Pie
Serves: 6

Old family recipe.

1 tablespoon	flour
1 cup	sugar
4	egg yolks
2 cups	milk
1 ½ squares	unsweetened chocolate
1 (9 inch)	graham cracker pie crust
4 teaspoons	cold water
1 package	unflavored gelatin
1 teaspoon	vanilla
1 teaspoon	butter or margarine
4	egg whites
½ cup	sugar

Mix flour and sugar. Add slightly beaten egg yolks and milk. Cook until thick; divide in half. To one half add shaved chocolate squares. Stir until chocolate melts. Pour into crust. To the other half, add the cold water in which the gelatin has been dissolved, vanilla and the butter. Stiffly beat the egg whites with the sugar and fold into custard mixture. Pour in crust over chocolate mixture. You may grate chocolate over top for garnish. Refrigerate overnight.

Chocolate Pecan Pie
Mary Agnes Hall
Serves: 8

2	eggs
1 cup	sugar
½ cup	flour
½ cup	butter or margarine, melted
1 teaspoon	vanilla
1 cup	pecans, coarsely chopped
6 ounces	semi-sweet chocolate pieces
1 (9 inch)	pastry shell, unbaked

Beat eggs slightly in a medium bowl. Blend in sugar, flour, butter and vanilla. Stir in pecans and chocolate pieces. Pour into pie shell. Bake at 325 degrees F. for 50 minutes or until lightly golden and firm on top. Cool on wire rack. Serve at room temperature.

Peggy Qualls

Sunken Soufflé Pie

Serves: 6-8

	butter
	bread crumbs
7 ounces	semi-sweet chocolate
¼ cup	water
6	egg yolks
8	egg whites
⅔ cup	sugar
1 cup	whipping cream
¼ cup	powdered sugar

Butter an 8 inch glass pie pan. Dust pan with bread crumbs. Place chocolate and water in the top part of a double boiler. Cook over medium heat until chocolate is melted. Stir until smooth. Cool to lukewarm. Add egg yolks, one at a time, into chocolate. Beat well after each addition. Beat egg whites and sugar at high speed until soft peaks form. By hand, stir one quarter of the egg whites into chocolate mixture to lighten it; then add the remaining egg whites. Fold only until no white shows, but do not overmix or the whites will deflate.

Reserve ¾ cup chocolate mixture, cover and put in refrigerator. Pour the remaining mixture into prepared pie pan; bake 25 minutes. Remove from oven and cool on rack. It will sink considerably. When soufflé completely cools, fill the sinkhole with the reserved mixture. Smooth out top. Whip cream at high speed until stiff. Add powdered sugar; beat until blended. Spread cream over top. Refrigerate at least 4 hours before serving.

Pat Tringas

Crum Bum Pie

¾ cup	powdered sugar
½ cup	crunchy peanut butter
3	eggs, separated
⅔ cup	sugar
½ teaspoon	salt
1 tablespoon	flour
¼ cup	cornstarch
3 cups	milk
2 tablespoons	butter, melted
1 teaspoon	vanilla
1 (9 inch)	pie shell, baked and cooled
¼ teaspoon	cream of tartar
⅓ cup	sugar

Blend together powdered sugar and peanut butter until it is a coarse, crumbled mixture; set aside. Beat egg yolks. In the top of a double boiler, combine sugar, salt, flour and cornstarch. Add milk. Cook over boiling water until mixture begins to thicken, stirring constantly. Add a little of the hot mixture to beaten egg yolks, then add yolks to milk mixture in double boiler. Continue to cook, stirring constantly until thick. Add melted butter and vanilla. Cover bottom of pie shell with ⅔ of the peanut butter crumble. Pour in the hot custard. In a clean bowl using spotlessly clean beaters, beat egg whites and cream of tartar until soft peaks form. At medium speed add sugar, 1 tablespoon at a time, scraping sugar from the sides of the bowl. Then beat egg whites at high speed until stiff. Place meringue on top of filling and spread out to edge of crust to seal. Sprinkle the remaining ⅓ of peanut butter crumble over the top. Bake at 350 degrees F. for 12-15 minutes or until meringue is golden.

Susan Lee

Ice Cream
Pie Spectacular

Serves: 8

This is an easy-to-fix, elegantly rich dessert. Sprinkle top with 1 cup crushed Heath Bars for garnish and added richness!

1	egg white
¼ teaspoon	salt
¼ cup	sugar
1½ cups	pecans, chopped
1 pint to 1 quart	coffee ice cream
1 pint to 1 quart	vanilla ice cream

Butter a 9 inch pie pan. Beat egg white until dry. Add salt and sugar. Fold in nuts. Spread in pie pan and prick with fork. Bake at 400 degrees F. for 10-12 minutes. Chill. Add ice cream in two layers. Cover and freeze. Serve with Caramel Sauce.

Caramel Sauce

3 tablespoons	butter
1 cup	light brown sugar
½ cup	heavy cream
1 teaspoon	vanilla

Heat butter; add sugar and cook for 10 minutes, stirring. Remove from heat and add cream slowly until blended. Heat 1 more minute. Add vanilla. Serve warm.

Lesley Blalock

228

Concord Grape Pie

Serves: 8

This is an old Kentucky recipe!

1 cup	Concord grapes
2 tablespoons	flour
2 tablespoons	water
4	egg yolks
½ cup	butter
1 cup	sugar
1 (9 inch)	pie pastry
4	egg whites

Skin and seed grapes. Mix flour and water. Beat egg yolks. Add yolks to flour and water mixture. Cream butter and sugar together and add to egg yolks, flour, and water mixture. Add grapes and mix carefully. Pour into an uncooked crust. Top with meringue made from the egg whites. Bake at 350 degrees F. until set.

Jean Blumer

Choconut Pie

Yield: 1 pie

3	eggs
¾ cup	sugar
¾ cup	dark corn syrup
1 teaspoon	vanilla
⅛ teaspoon	salt
¼ cup	margarine, melted
1 tablespoon	cocoa
2 cups	pecan halves
½ cup	shredded coconut
1 (9-inch)	pie pastry

Combine eggs, sugar, syrup, vanilla and salt. Combine margarine and cocoa, stirring into above mixture. Add pecans and coconut, mixing well. Pour mixture into pie pastry. Bake at 350 degrees F. about 50 minutes or until set.

Sugar Mill Sweets

Yogurt Pie

A light and fluffy dessert.

24	Ritz crackers
¼ teaspoon	baking powder
½ cup	pecans, finely chopped
1 teaspoon	vanilla
3	egg whites
1 cup	sugar

Crush Ritz crackers until fine. Add baking powder, pecans and vanilla. Beat egg whites until stiff; add sugar. Fold cracker mixture into egg whites. Pour into a buttered 9 inch pie pan. Bake at 325 degrees F. for 30 minutes. Cool.

FILLING

1 (10 ounce) container	frozen strawberries, thawed
1 carton	strawberry yogurt
1 (8 ounce) carton	whipped topping

Crush and drain strawberries. Fold yogurt into whipped topping and add strawberries. Pour into cooled pie crust. Chill.

Sandy Benton

Lime Cheese Pie

CRUST

15 slices	Zwieback
¼ cup	slivered almonds
⅓ cup	sugar
⅓ cup	butter, melted
¼ teaspoon	cinnamon

Place ⅓ of the Zwieback and ⅓ of the almonds in blender; blend on high speed until Zwieback is finely crushed. Remove to bowl. Repeat process twice. Add sugar, butter and cinnamon to crumb mixture; blend well. Press mixture into a 10-inch pie pan, reserving 1 tablespoon of mixture for garnish. Bake crust at 375 degrees F. for 8 minutes.

FILLING

½ cup	milk
2 tablespoons	unflavored gelatin
2 thin strips	lime peel
dash	salt
½ cup	lime juice
¾ cup	sugar
2	eggs
few drops	green food coloring
1 (8 ounce) package	cream cheese
1 cup	chopped ice
1 cup	light cream
1 cup	cream, whipped
	sugar

Scald the milk. Combine milk, gelatin, lime peel, salt and juice in blender. Blend, covered, on high speed for 1 minute. Add sugar, eggs, food coloring and cream cheese. Blend, covered, on high speed for 15 seconds. With motor running, add ice. Add light cream. Blend for 10 seconds or until well mixed. Let stand for 2 minutes or until slightly thickened. Pour into prepared crust; chill until set. Top with whipped cream sweetened with additional sugar. Garnish with reserved crumbs and lime twists, if desired.

Barbara Balcanof

Peaches And Cream Pie

Serves: 6

1 (8 ounce) package	cream cheese, softened
2 tablespoons	milk
½ teaspoon	almond extract
2 tablespoons	sugar
1	baked pie shell, either graham cracker or pastry
1 (1 pound 15 ounce) can	sliced peaches, drained, reserve liquid

Mix cream cheese, milk, almond extract and sugar together until well blended. Spread into a fully prepared pastry shell. Chill. Arrange peach slices on top of pie filling.

Glaze

1 tablespoon	cornstarch
¼ cup	sugar
1 tablespoon	lemon juice
⅔ cup	peach juice
1 tablespoon	margarine

Combine all ingredients except margarine in a small saucepan. Cook over medium heat, stirring constantly. When thick and clear, add margarine and cook 2 more minutes. When cool, pour over peaches. Cool approximately 2 hours before serving.

Lyn Sheffield

Strawberry Heaven

Serves: 6-8

BUTTER COCONUT CRUST

6 tablespoons	butter, unsalted
2½ cups	coconut flakes, lightly packed

Melt butter in a saucepan; stir in coconut flakes. Press into an 8 or 9 inch pie pan. Bake at 325 degrees F. for 20 minutes or until lightly browned. Chill until ready to use.

FILLING

1½ pints	fresh strawberries
¾ cup	sugar
1 tablespoon	rum
1 envelope	unflavored gelatin
½ cup	water
1 cup	heavy cream, chilled or 1 (8 ounce) container whipped topping

Wash, hull and slice strawberries. Reserve a few slices for garnish. Mix the remaining strawberry slices with sugar and rum. Let stand at room temperature 10 minutes; stir twice. Meanwhile, soften gelatin in water, then stir over medium-low heat until dissolved; cool. Add gelatin to the strawberry mixture; set aside. Using a cold bowl, whip cream until stiff. Fold into strawberry mixture. Chill the mixture 45 minutes, stirring twice. Pour into chilled crust. Chill again at least 4 hours before serving. Garnish with reserved strawberry slices.

Pat Tringas

Muh's Cherry Pudding
Serves: 16

Excellent sweet treat for the 4th of July.

1 quart can	semi-sweet seedless cherries
	flour
2	eggs
1 cup	sugar
1 tablespoon	butter
1 cup	milk
2 cups	flour
1 heaping tablespoon	baking powder

Drain cherries and roll in enough flour to coat. Place in the bottom of a greased 9 inch tube pan. Beat eggs and blend in sugar and butter. Add milk. Beat in dry ingredients. Pour over cherries in tube pan. Bake at 375 degrees F. for 45 minutes. Remove from pan and cool. Refrigerate. When serving, spread hard sauce over individual pieces.

Hard Sauce

½ cup	butter, softened
1 box	powdered sugar
1 teaspoon	vanilla

Combine butter and sugar until creamy; add vanilla. Refrigerate.

Sandy Benton

Greek

Greek

Greek heritage and tradition is very rich in the area along Northwest Florida's gulf coast. One of the first pioneer families to this region was Greek. They started a ship-building industry which created many jobs and attracted even more Greeks from the old country. Ships from this family business were used locally in the fishing industry and farther south in the sponging industry.

As the Greek population grew in Northwest Florida, so did the area's economy grow. Taxi services, banks, newspapers, theaters and motels are among the Greek-owned businesses which helped the area to prosper.

Today, Greek influence and tradition still thrive in our fast-paced life. This coastal area is known for its fine fishing fleet and many restaurants which are Greek owned and operated. We are proud to have them share a collection of their families' favorite recipes.

Appetizer Platter

A traditional Greek platter of appetizers may include a variety of the following: Feta cheese, Kasseri cheese, Mezithra cheese, cucumber slices or sticks, tomato wedges, Calamatra or black olives, Salonika peppers, anchovy filets, artichoke hearts marinated in lemon and oil, stuffed grape leaves and Greek meatballs. Ouzo and goblets of water are served.

Tangy Cognac Shrimp   *Serves: 4*

This is perfect as a first course or may be served with crusty bread and a salad. Freezes well. Defrost and bake covered at 400 degrees F. for 10 to 15 minutes.

1 (28 ounce) can	tomatoes
6 tablespoons	olive oil
1 medium	onion, finely chopped
1 clove	garlic, finely minced
¼ teaspoon	sugar
	salt and pepper to taste
2 tablespoons	butter
2 pounds	raw shrimp, peeled and deveined
3 tablespoons	Ouzo (Greek liquor)
3 tablespoons	Metaxa cognac
¼ pound	Feta cheese
2 tablespoons	fresh parsley, chopped

Pour tomatoes into a mixing bowl. Squeeze into small pieces. Heat 4 tablespoons oil in heavy saucepan. Lightly sauté onions and garlic. Add tomatoes, sugar, salt and pepper. Cook, uncovered, over medium heat until sauce is thickened. Heat butter and 2 remaining tablespoons oil in a large, heavy skillet. Sauté shrimp over medium heat until pink. Add Ouzo and cognac. Flame shrimp. Place in casserole or individual ramekins. Cover with the tomato sauce mixture. Sprinkle with crumbled Feta cheese and parsley. Bake at 425 degrees F. for 10 minutes or until well heated and Feta has melted.

Dixie Aftonomos

Dolmas
(Stuffed Grapeleaves)

Serves: 8-10

1½ pounds	lean ground beef
2 cups	raw long-grain rice
1 medium	onion, finely chopped
¾ cup	olive oil
3 tablespoons	crushed, dried mint
1 teaspoon	salt
1 teaspoon	pepper
1 (6 ounce) can	tomato paste
1 (18 ounce) jar	grapevine leaves in brine
1 large	lemon

Combine the first 8 ingredients in a large bowl. Use hands to mix thoroughly. Remove the first two rolls of grape leaves from jar. Unroll and rinse in cold water. Drain. Line the bottom of a 3 quart pot with 3 or 4 leaves. Lay a leaf, vein-side up, with stem pointing towards you. Place a teaspoon of filling on the leaf where the stem begins. Fold the bottom two points of the leaf over the filling. Tuck in side edges. Roll tightly. Place in bottom of pot. Continue to fill pot with stuffed leaves. Place them tightly together in concentric circles, layer upon layer. When pot is full, slowly pour in enough cold water to barely cover stuffed leaves. Squeeze the juice of 1 large lemon over this. Weigh down the leaves with a sandwich plate or saucer that fits inside the pot. Cover the pot and bring to a slow boil. Simmer about 1½ hours or until the rice is tender. Add more water as necessary. When done, remove from heat. Let sit in covered pot 15 minutes before serving.

Augolemono Sauce

2	eggs, separated
	juice of 2 lemons

Beat egg whites until stiff and add egg yolks. Beat until blended. Beat in lemon juice just until mixed. Ladle sauce over servings of stuffed grapeleaves.

Helen Aftonomos

Triopetes
(Cheese Triangles)

Yield: 4 dozen

1 (3 ounce) package	cream cheese, softened
½ pound	Feta cheese, crumbled
½ pound	cottage cheese
3	eggs
1 pound	phyllo
1½ cups	butter, melted

Combine cheeses and stir. Add eggs, one at a time, and mix well. Cut each phyllo pastry sheet into 3 inch lengthwise strips. Brush each with melted butter. Place 1 teaspoon of filling on one end of the strip and fold pastry over to make a triangle. Continue folding from side to side in a triangular form. Proceed this way for the length of each strip. Place the triangles on a buttered cookie sheet. Brush tops with melted butter. Bake at 325 degrees F. until lightly browned. Serve as appetizers.

Stella Benaquis

Taramosalata
(Greek Caviar)

Yield: 2 cups

A Greek Easter favorite!

4 ounces	fish roe (tarama)
	juice of 2 lemons
8 slices	day-old bread, moistened in water
½ cup	olive oil

Blend fish roe with half of the lemon juice in mixer thoroughly. Meanwhile, trim crusts from the bread. Continue beating fish roe mixture, adding alternately small pieces of bread, olive oil and remaining lemon juice. Mixture should thicken to the consistency of thick mayonnaise. Serve as a dip with crackers or in the center of a salad tray, ringed with slices of green pepper, tomatoes, cucumbers, lettuce and olives.

Andrea Liollio Georgiades

Vasilopita
(New Year's Bread)

Yield: 2 loaves

A coin is baked with this bread. The person who receives the slice of bread with the coin has good luck for the new year.

2½ pounds	flour
1 teaspoon	salt
	mixed whole spices (cinnamon, cloves, nutmeg, anise, allspice)
	water
1 cup	butter, melted
1½ cups	milk
6	eggs, at room temperature
2 cups	sugar
4 cakes	compressed yeast
½ cup	water, lukewarm
	butter, melted
1	egg yolk
1 tablespoon	water

Place flour in a large bowl, making a well in the center. Add salt and set aside. Boil spices in water; strain and reserve ½ cup liquid. Melt butter in milk; add ½ cup liquid from boiled spices and heat to lukewarm. Gradually pour all liquids into center of flour well. In a separate bowl, beat eggs slightly; add sugar and mix until dissolved. Gradually add this mixture to the center of the flour well and stir together with other ingredients. Crumble yeast cakes in lukewarm water and add to the mixture. Mix in a circular motion to blend all the ingredients. Place on floured board and knead thoroughly. Dough will be soft but not sticky when ready. While kneading, rub hands with butter to prevent sticking. When dough is ready, brush surface with melted butter; cover and allow to rise in a warm place. Knead a second time; cover and let rise. Repeat again. The dough must rise three times. After the third time, place a coin wrapped in waxed paper inside dough. Shape and place into desired baking pans. Brush tops with a mixture of egg yolk and water. Bake at 375 degrees F. for 15 minutes; reduce heat to 325 degrees F. and bake for another 15-20 minutes or until golden brown.

Nancy Papantonis

Easter Bread

Hard-cooked eggs, dyed red, are a Greek tradition at Easter time. Two or three of these brightly colored eggs are nestled into each anise braid before baking. This symbolizes good luck for the household. A favorite family game is for everyone to grasp one of the red eggs tightly in his hand with the point showing. Each tries to crack the other's egg. The winner is the lucky one who successfully escapes having his egg cracked.

1 package	dry yeast
¼ cup	water, heated to 105°-115°
⅓ cup	sugar
¼ cup	butter, softened
½ teaspoon	salt
½ cup	milk
¼ teaspoon	oil of anise
5 drops	oil of cinnamon
2¾ to 3 cups	flour
2	eggs
1 tablespoon	water
3 tablespoons	sesame seeds

Sprinkle yeast over water; mix until dissolved. In large bowl combine sugar, butter and salt. Heat milk to scalding. Pour over contents in bowl. Stir until butter melts. Cool to lukewarm. Add anise and cinnamon. Stir in 1 cup flour and beat well. Add 1 beaten egg and dissolved yeast. Beat well. Gradually mix in remaining flour to make a soft dough. Place dough on floured surface and cover. Let rest 10 minutes. Knead until smooth or 8-10 minutes. Shape dough into ball. Place in lightly oiled bowl. Turn to grease all sides. Cover and set in a warm place for about 1½ hours until doubled in size. Punch down and cover bowl. Return to warm place. Let rise until doubled again. Place on floured surface; divide into three equal parts and shape each into a ball. Let rest 10 minutes. Grease baking sheet and set aside. Roll each dough ball into an 18 inch rope, tapering ends. Line ropes 1 inch apart on baking sheet. Working from middle to each end, loosely braid ropes. Pinch ends together and tuck under slightly. Cover and let rise in a warm place about 45 minutes or until doubled. Beat water and remaining egg together. Brush over braid. Sprinkle with sesame seeds. Bake at 375 degrees F. for about 25 minutes or until deep brown. Cool slightly before serving.

Dixie Aftonomos

Grecian
Lemon Nut Bread

Yield: 1 loaf

¾ cup	butter or margarine, softened
1½ cups	sugar
3	eggs
2¼ cups	flour
¼ teaspoon	salt
¼ teaspoon	baking soda
¼ cup	buttermilk
	rind of 1 lemon, grated
¾ cup	pecans, chopped
	juice of 2 lemons
¾ cup	powdered sugar

Combine butter and sugar; cream until light and fluffy. Add eggs, beating well. Combine dry ingredients. Add buttermilk and dry ingredients alternately to sugar mixture, beginning and ending with buttermilk. Stir just until all ingredients are moistened. Stir in lemon rind and pecans. Spoon batter into a greased 9 x 5 x 3 inch loaf pan. Bake at 325 degrees F. for 1¼ hours or until bread tests done. Combine lemon juice and powdered sugar; stir well. Punch holes in top of warm bread. Pour on glaze. Cool on wire rack.

Tasia Davis

Hearty Moussaka

Serves: 8

10	potatoes
5	eggplants
	oil
	salt and pepper to taste

MEAT SAUCE

1½ pounds	ground meat
3 tablespoons	oil
2-3	onions, chopped
3-4 cloves	garlic, minced
	salt and pepper to taste
1 (16 ounce) can	tomato juice

CREAM SAUCE

4 cups	milk
6 teaspoons	cornstarch
1 teaspoon	salt
¼ cup	butter
4	egg yolks

Peel and slice potatoes lengthwise. Slice eggplant lengthwise. Sauté potatoes and eggplant separately in oil until lightly browned. Place in layers on paper towels and drain well. Cover bottom of baking dish with a layer of half the potatoes; season with salt and pepper. Add layer of half the eggplant and season also with salt and pepper. Prepare meat sauce by sautéing ground meat in oil. Add onions, garlic, salt and pepper. Simmer for 10-15 minutes. Stir in tomato juice and simmer for 30 minutes. After that time, pour meat sauce over top of eggplant. Repeat layers and seasoning, using all the vegetables. Prepare cream sauce by pouring milk in saucepan and stirring in cornstarch until dissolved. Place over medium heat, stirring constantly, until mixture comes to a boil and thickens. Stir in salt; remove from heat. Add butter and stir until melted. Add egg yolks, 1 at a time, stirring well after each addition. Pour cream sauce over the top of eggplant and spread evenly. Bake in preheated 400 degree F. oven until vegetables are tender and sauce is golden brown.

Nina Michas

Pastitso

Serves: 10

Serve with tossed salad. Pastitso freezes well. Thaw before reheating at 400 degrees F. for 20-30 minutes. Pastitso is the Greek version of lasagna. It consists of layers of elbow macaroni, Parmesan cheese and spicy meat filling, all held together by a rich cream sauce.

MEAT LAYER	1 tablespoon	butter
	1 medium	onion, finely chopped
	3 pounds	ground beef
	1 (6 ounce) can	tomato paste
	¾ cup	water
	1½ teaspoons	salt
	¼ teaspoon	pepper
	¼ teaspoon	nutmeg
	2	eggs, well beaten
MACARONI LAYER	1½ pounds	elbow macaroni
	2	eggs, well beaten
	1 cup	Parmesan cheese, grated
	½ cup	butter, melted
CREAM SAUCE LAYER	4	eggs
	¾ cup	milk
	1 cup	Parmesan cheese, grated
	1 tablespoon	flour
	½ teaspoon	salt
		nutmeg

Heat butter in frying pan. Sauté onion. Add meat and sauté until evenly browned. Stir in tomato paste, water, salt, pepper and nutmeg. Cover and simmer 5 minutes. Uncover and simmer another 5 minutes. Remove from heat. Adjust salt to taste and refrigerate. When cool, remove any traces of congealed fat. Mix in eggs and set aside.

Cook macaroni according to directions and drain. Put half of macaroni in a bowl and add eggs. After mixing, spread in an 11 x 14 x 2 inch baking pan. Sprinkle with ½ cup Parmesan cheese. Spread meat mixture over macaroni. Arrange remaining macaroni over meat layer. Sprinkle with remaining ½ cup Parmesan. Pour butter over Parmesan layer.

To prepare cream sauce, beat eggs to a froth. Blend in milk, cheese, flour and salt. Pour over meat and macaroni layers. Sprinkle lightly with nutmeg. Cover with foil. Bake at 400 degrees F. for 15 minutes. Remove foil. Bake 45 minutes longer or until golden brown. Remove from oven. Wait 15 minutes before cutting.

Helen Aftonomos

Keftethes
(Greek Meatballs)

These are also delicious when eaten with freshly squeezed lemon juice.

1 teaspoon	ground allspice
5 tablespoons	parsley, chopped
3 tablespoons	spearmint leaves or dried mint, chopped
2 tablespoons	salt
½ teaspoon	pepper
¾ pound	ground lamb or 1 pound ground beef
¾ pound	ground beef or ½ pound ground pork
3 slices	bread, soaked in water and gently squeezed
2	eggs
2	onions, chopped
3 cloves	garlic, minced
	flour
	oil

Combine spices and sprinkle over meat. Add remaining ingredients except flour and oil; allow to stand for 1-2 hours. Roll into balls; dip in flour and fry in hot oil until golden. Can be made small, dipped in tomato sauce and served as hors d'oeuvres.

Gus Lucas

Spanakopita (Spinach Pie)

Serves: 18

A variation is to prepare as appetizers by making triangles and placing unbaked in the freezer. Prior to serving, remove from the freezer; allow to thaw a little, bake and serve warm.

¼ cup	butter or margarine
½ cup	onion, finely chopped
3 (10 ounce) packages	frozen chopped spinach, thawed
3	eggs
½ pound	Feta cheese, crumbled
½ cup	parsley, chopped
1 teaspoon	salt
⅛ teaspoon	pepper
1 cup	butter or margarine, melted
1 pound	phyllo pastry

Preheat oven to 350 degrees F. Place ¼ cup butter in a medium saucepan. Sauté onion in butter until golden, about 5 minutes. Add spinach; stir well. Remove from heat. In a large bowl beat eggs, cheese, parsley, salt and pepper and spinach-onion mixture. Mix well. Brush a 13 x 9 x 2 inch baking pan lightly with melted butter. Layer 8 phyllo pastry leaves, and brush the top of each with melted butter. Spread evenly with spinach mixture. Cover with 8 more leaves, brushing each with butter. Cut through top pastry layer to form 18 rectangles about 3 x 2 inches. Bake 30-35 minutes or until top crust is puffy and golden.

TRIANGLES

Cut each pastry sheet into 3 inch strips. Brush with melted butter. Place 1 teaspoon of the filling on one end of the strip and fold over to make a triangle. Continue folding from side to side in the form of a triangle. Proceed this way for length of strip. Bake on greased cookie sheet for 30-35 minutes at 350 degrees F., turning after brown on one side, approximately 15 minutes.

Tasia Davis

Individual Stuffed Eggplant

Serves: 8

8 small	eggplants
1 tablespoon	butter
2	onions, finely chopped
1 pound	chopped meat
	parsley
	salt and pepper to taste
1	egg
¼ cup	milk
½ cup	grated cheese

Cut eggplants lengthwise and scoop out pulp from center. Sauté onions in butter. Add pulp of the eggplant and then add the meat. Add parsley, salt and pepper. Cook for about 10 minutes. Stuff the eggplant shells with the mixture and bake at 350 degrees F. for 30 minutes. While they are baking, beat together egg and milk; add grated cheese. Season to taste. Remove eggplants from oven and cover each with cheese sauce. Place under broiler until brown. Serve at once.

Joy Hanshaw

Dessert Platter

The standard Greek dessert is not pastry but a platter of fruits, nuts and cheese. Arrange any of the following, as desired: cantaloupe and honeydew melon, grapes, apricots, watermelon chunks, peaches or nectarines, pomegranates, Feta cheese, Kasseri cheese, almonds and walnuts in their shells, pistachios, dried Calamata crown figs, dried dates, dark and currant raisins and dried apricots.

Karithopita
(Greek Nut Cake)

This recipe is delicious any time of the year, but it lasts longer in the fall and winter months. After 5 days it should be refrigerated. The cake can be frozen without the glaze. Pour hot glaze over cake after it has thawed. Prepare a day ahead so the flavors can blend.

¾ cup	butter
1 cup	sugar
6	eggs, separated
½ box	Zwieback, grated or finely crushed
1 teaspoon	baking powder
½ teaspoon	ground cinnamon
½ teaspoon	ground cloves
½ teaspoon	vanilla
	rind of 1 orange, grated
	rind of ½ lemon, grated
1 tablespoon	whiskey (bourbon or blend)
2 cups	chopped pecans

Cream butter and sugar until light and fluffy. Add egg yolks, beating slowly. Add Zwieback, baking powder, spices, vanilla, rinds and whiskey, beating slowly until well-mixed. Add pecans and mix. Fold in stiffly-beaten egg whites. Pour mixture into buttered 11 x 13 x 2-inch pan. Bake at 350 degrees F. for 30-40 minutes. Punch holes in cake with toothpick or cake tester. Let cool until glaze is prepared.

Glaze

¾ cup	sugar
½ cup	water
1 teaspoon	lemon juice

Mix all ingredients in a saucepan over low heat and stir until sugar is dissolved. Bring to a boil and lower heat to simmer. Simmer for 30 minutes. Pour hot syrup over cake and cool completely. Cut into diamonds or squares.

Mary N. Coumanis

Baklava

2 pounds	ground pecans
1 teaspoon	cinnamon
½ pound	ground roasted almonds
1 teaspoon	powdered cloves
1 cup	sugar
1 teaspoon	nutmeg
2 cups	butter or margarine, melted
1 pound	phyllo (pastry sheets)
3 cups	sugar
1½ cups	water
3 strips	lemon peel
3 sticks	cinnamon
1 dozen	whole cloves
½ cup	honey

Preheat oven to 300 degrees F. Combine pecans, cinnamon, almonds, cloves, sugar and nutmeg. Set aside. Brush a shallow pan with melted butter. Place 8 sheets of the phyllo on bottom of pan, brushing with butter between each layer. Sprinkle with 1/3 of the filling mixture. Place 4 sheets of phyllo on top of this, being sure to butter between each layer. Sprinkle with 1/3 more of the filling. Place another 4 sheets of phyllo and sprinkle the remainder of the filling over it. Put 8 sheets on top. Always be sure to brush between each phyllo sheet with melted butter. Brush top with butter; cut in squares or diamond shapes. Bake for 1 hour or until well browned. While baking, combine sugar, water, lemon peel, cinnamon and cloves. Bring to a boil and add honey. Boil for 5 minutes. Pour through a strainer over the Baklava as soon as the Baklava is removed from the oven.

Tasia Davis

Kolokethopita
(Pumpkin Dessert)

Serves: 16-18

10 cups	fresh ground pumpkin
1 tablespoon	salt
¼ cup	oil
1 cup	sweet butter, melted
½ cup	sugar
1 cup	white raisins
1 teaspoon	cinnamon
¼ teaspoon	cloves
2 cups	walnuts or pecans, chopped
1 pound	phyllo

Place ground pumpkin in a towel; sprinkle with salt. Allow to stand overnight to remove water. Put pumpkin in pan, add oil and ¼ cup butter. Simmer 1 hour, stirring often to prevent scorching. Add sugar, raisins, cinnamon and cloves during the last 5 minutes of simmering time. Remove from heat and add 1 cup of nuts. Allow mixture to cool. Brush the bottom of a 13 x 9 x 2 inch pan with melted butter. Layer 3 sheets of phyllo, making sure each is brushed with butter. Sprinkle with a few nuts. Layer 3 more sheets of phyllo, brushing each with butter. Sprinkle with a few more nuts. Pour pumpkin mixture on top of layered phyllo. Cover with remaining phyllo, brushing each layer with melted butter (about 6 layers). Bake at 375 degrees F. for 10-15 minutes. Lower oven to 350 degrees F. and bake 45 minutes.

SYRUP

3 cups	sugar
2 cups	water
1 stick	cinnamon
1 slice	lemon

Combine all ingredients in a saucepan and bring to a boil. Simmer for 10-15 minutes. Cool syrup and pour over Kolokethopita when taken out of oven. Cut in squares.

Saundra Tashik

Kourambiedes (Powdered Sugar Cookies)

Yield: 10 dozen

4 cups	butter
½ cup	powdered sugar, sifted
2 tablespoons	whiskey
2 teaspoons	vanilla
½ teaspoon	orange extract
2	egg yolks
5-5½ cups	flour, sifted
1 (16 ounce) box	powdered sugar

Beat butter and ½ cup powdered sugar until butter is white in color. Add remaining ingredients except sugar. Dough should feel a little sticky, but workable. Place brown paper (such as grocery bag paper) on a cookie sheet. Drop in 1 teaspoon-size mounds two inches apart on papered cookie sheet. Bake at 350 degrees F. for ½ hour or until golden brown. Sprinkle with lots of powdered sugar immediately upon removing from oven. Serve in soufflé cups or individual aluminum cups.

Saundra Tashik

Greek Coffee

Serves: 4

Greek coffee is served in taverns in Greece and traditionally, after dinner, with a glass of cognac. It is made in small brass coffee makers and served in demitasse cups. Greek coffee is extremely strong and is meant for leisurely sipping. The sign of a well-made cup is the foam floating on the top of the coffee.

4 demitasse cups	cold water
1 (4 cup)	long-handled Greek coffee maker
4 teaspoons, level	sugar
4 teaspoons, rounded	Turkish coffee

Pour 4 demitasse cups of cold water into coffee maker. Bring to a boil. Add sugar and stir until dissolved. Maintain boiling temperature. Add coffee and stir well. Remove coffee maker immediately from heat. A foam should appear on the surface of the coffee. Pour a little of this foam evenly into each of the 4 demitasse cups; then carefully fill the cups with the remaining coffee. Serve immediately.

Dixie Aftonomos

Restaurants

Restaurants

Pat See-Iw (Fried Noodles With Beef And Broccoli)

½ cup	oil
½ tablespoon	garlic
½ cup	sirloin steak, thinly sliced
¾ cup	fresh broccoli, sliced
1 cup	rice noodles
1 tablespoon	Chinese soy sauce
½ tablespoon	nampla

Heat oil in a frying pan. Brown garlic until light brown. Add sliced beef and stir-fry for 2 minutes. Add broccoli, turning over a few times. Add the rice noodles, soy sauce and nampla. Stir-fry until noodles are brown. Place on a serving plate. Serve hot.

Bangkok House

Shrimp, Scallop And Steak Sauté

4 large	shrimp, peeled and deveined
4 large	scallops
4 cubes (1 ounce each)	beef tenderloin
½ ounce	green pepper, diced
½ ounce	red pepper, diced
½ ounce	onion, diced
1 ounce	mushrooms, quartered
⅛ teaspoon	garlic
2 ounces	soy sauce
⅛ teaspoon	ginger

In a hot sauté pan, add beef and brown quickly. Add seafood and vegetables; sauté until done. Add garlic, ginger and soy sauce. Serve over rice.

**Bayview Dining Room
at Sandestin Beach Resort**

Coquille St. Jacques

Serves: 4

2 pounds	sea scallops, rinsed and patted dry
	flour for dredging
¼ cup	soybean oil
2 tablespoons	unsalted butter
1 tablespoon	flour
1 cup	white fish stock or ¾ cup bottled clam juice and ¼ cup dry white wine
3 small cloves	garlic, minced
⅓ cup	heavy cream
¼ cup	fresh lemon juice
¼ cup	stewed tomatoes
sprinkle	white pepper
	salt to taste
	fresh parsley, chopped

Dredge scallops in flour; shake off excess. In a stainless steel skillet, heat the oil over high heat until it is smoking. Sauté scallops for 3 minutes and transfer them to a heavy saucepan. Pour off the oil; reduce heat to low and add butter to the skillet. Stir in the flour and cook, stirring for 1 minute. Warm the fish stock and add in a stream, whisking until it is smooth. Add garlic; simmer sauce for 2 minutes. Add cream; simmer and stir in lemon juice, tomatoes, white pepper and salt. Strain the sauce through a fine sieve over the scallops. Bring the sauce to a simmer over moderate heat. Transfer to a heated serving dish. Garnish with chopped parsley.

Bay Cafe

Fish Milanese

Bayou Bill's
Harbor Side Restaurant and Oyster Bar

Serves: 3-4

⅓ cup + 2 tablespoons	olive oil
2 tablespoons	lemon juice
½ teaspoon	salt
dash	pepper
1 small	onion, finely chopped
1 pound	grouper
2 large	eggs
1 tablespoon	milk
¾ cup	fine, dry, unseasoned bread crumbs
½ cup	flour
¼ cup	butter
1 clove	garlic, minced

Whisk ⅓ cup of the oil, lemon juice, salt and pepper in a small bowl. Stir in onion. Transfer marinade to non-corrosive baking dish. Place fish in marinade. Refrigerate for 1 hour. Whisk egg and milk in a bowl. Spread bread crumbs and flour on separate plates. Dip fish first in flour, then in eggs, then in bread crumbs. Heat 2 tablespoons of the butter and remaining oil in large skillet over medium heat. Add fish. Cook, turning once, until golden brown, about 2-3 minutes. Melt remaining butter in skillet. Add garlic. Cook until butter turns light brown. Pour browned butter over fish. Serve at once.

Bayou Bill's

Blue Room's World Famous Cheese Sauce

2½ pounds	Velveeta cheese
½ pound	butter, melted
½ cup	onion, finely chopped
2 tablespoons	chives
¼ teaspoon	garlic powder
2-4 tablespoons	lemon juice (to taste)

Melt cheese in double boiler. Stir in remaining ingredients until smooth. Serve sauce over baked oysters or in your favorite seafood casserole.

Blue Room Restaurant

Oil And Vinegar Dressing

Yield: 1 gallon

½ gallon	olive oil
¾ quart	tarragon vinegar
8 ounces	Dijon-style mustard
4 ounces	honey
4	green onions, diced
2 ounces	sweet red peppers, diced
5 tablespoons	dill weed
1 tablespoon	garlic salt

Combine ingredients and chill. Serve over mixed greens.

Chan's

Salmon Mousse

Serves: 6-8

1 package	unflavored gelatin
3 tablespoons	lemon juice
½ cup	boiling water
½ cup	mayonnaise
2 cups	cooked salmon or
	1 (16 ounce) can, drained
¼ teaspoon	paprika
1 teaspoon	dill, chopped
1 cup	heavy cream
	watercress
	thin lemon slices

Combine the gelatin, lemon juice and boiling water in a blender and blend at high speed for 40 seconds. Add the mayonnaise, salmon, paprika and dill and blend briefly. Add cream while blending for 30 seconds more. Pour into a 4-cup mold. Chill until mousse is set. Turn mold onto a serving platter. Garnish with watercress and lemon slices.

**Coral Reef at
Marina Bay Resort**

Teriyaki Sauce

1 tablespoon	water
1 tablespoon	soy sauce
1 tablespoon	Worcestershire sauce
2 tablespoons	pineapple juice
1½ teaspoons	sherry
pinch	ginger
	garlic salt to taste

Combine all ingredients. Mix well.

Destinees'

Huntington Dressing

2 cups	white vinegar
1 cup	salad oil
1 small	onion, grated
1 cup	sugar
½ cup	Worcestershire sauce
dash	cayenne pepper

Mix all ingredients and stir well. This "house" dressing is served over mixed greens or spinach.

Earthsongs Cafe

West Indies Salad

1 pound	lump crabmeat, fresh
½ cup	cider vinegar
½ cup	salad oil
½ cup	ice water
1	onion, finely chopped
	salt to taste
	lemon-pepper to taste

Combine salt, pepper, onion, oil, vinegar and water. Pour over crabmeat and let stand for several hours.

**Finnegan's
Dockside Cafe**

Cauliflower With Water Chestnuts

HUNAN II
CHINESE RESTAURANT
& LOUNGE

Serves: 6

1 head	cauliflower, cut into flowerets
¼ cup	chicken broth
1 tablespoon	sherry
1 tablespoon	soy sauce
½ teaspoon	cornstarch
1 tablespoon	cold water
2 tablespoons	cooking oil
1 tablespoon	fresh ginger, minced
1 (8 ounce) can	water chestnuts, thinly sliced
2	green onions, minced
¼ cup	cooked ham, minced

Blanch cauliflower flowerets in boiling, salted water to cover for 3 minutes. Drain in colander and rinse with cold water to stop cooking. In a small bowl, combine chicken broth, sherry and soy sauce; set aside. In another small bowl, blend cornstarch and cold water; set aside. Place wok or large skillet over medium high heat. When it is hot, add 2 tablespoons cooking oil. Add ginger and cook, stirring, until it is golden, about 30 seconds. Add water chestnuts and green onion; cook, stirring until heated through, or about 1 minute. Add cauliflower, a cup at a time, stirring and turning each addition so that the flowerets become coated with oil. Add chicken broth mixture and bring to a boil. Reduce heat to moderate and simmer vegetable mixture 2 minutes or until cauliflower is tender-crisp. Stir cornstarch mixture and add to pan. Continue cooking and stirring until sauce has thickened and has thoroughly coated cauliflower. Place vegetables in serving bowl and top with minced ham. Serve immediately.

Hunan II

Conch Chowder

6½ cups	canned tomatoes, peeled
3	onions, diced
6	carrots, peeled and sliced
4	potatoes, peeled and sliced
3	jalapeño peppers, sliced
2 tablespoons	beef-flavored bouillon
5 pounds	conch
1 cup	butter, melted
3¼ cups	canned corn
	salt to taste
13 cups	water

In a large pot break up tomatoes. Add onion, carrots, potatoes, jalapeño peppers and beef bouillon. Cook until tender. Clean conch; mince and sauté in butter. Add to tomato mixture. Stir in corn, water and salt. Cook until it boils.

Harbor Docks

Crawfish Fettuccine

Serves: 4

1 pound	crawfish tails, peeled
2 ounces	butter
1 clove	garlic, chopped
1 pound	fettuccine noodles
4 ounces	heavy cream
4 ounces	Parmesan cheese, grated
	fresh parsley, chopped

Sauté crawfish tails in butter and garlic for 1-2 minutes and set aside. Cook fettuccine according to package instructions and drain. In a sauté pan, add heavy cream and cheese to cooled fettuccine and toss over medium heat until hot. Add crawfish and toss to evenly distribute over the tails. Divide into servings and sprinkle with chopped parsley.

J P's Cafe
Holiday Inn
Ft. Walton Beach

Chicken Islander

Serves: 4

8	chicken breasts, boned
½ cup	butter, melted
¼ cup	lemon juice
1 teaspoon	garlic salt

Islander Sauce

1 pound	Velveeta cheese
½ cup	Half and Half
½ cup	white wine
1 teaspoon	celery seed
1 teaspoon	white pepper
2 cups	popcorn shrimp, boiled, peeled and deveined
	parsley, chopped

Bake chicken breasts with melted butter, lemon juice and garlic salt in a 2-inch deep pan at 375 degrees F. for 20-25 minutes. While chicken is baking, melt cheese with Half and Half until well-blended. Add wine, celery seed, pepper and shrimp. Stir gently. To serve, place 2 chicken breasts in each of four individual casserole dishes and pour Islander Sauce over chicken. Return to oven and brown top lightly (approximately 5 minutes at 450 degrees F.). Garnish dishes with finely chopped parsley.

Jamaica Joe's

Chicken Mornay

The Landing

Serves: 6-8

1 (10 ounce) package	French style green beans, frozen
	salt
¼ cup	butter
5 tablespoons	flour
2 cubes	chicken or beef-flavored bouillon
½ cup	heavy cream
¼ teaspoon	salt
dash	pepper
1 teaspoon	Worcestershire sauce
1 (10 ounce) can	mushrooms, drained
¼ cup	sherry
2 cups	chicken or beef, cooked and cut in small pieces
¼ cup	slivered almonds, toasted
⅓ cup	Parmesan cheese, grated

Partially cook beans in boiling, salted water; drain. Melt butter in saucepan; blend in flour. Dissolve bouillon cubes in water or use chicken or beef broth. Gradually add bouillon and cream to flour mixture. Cook over medium heat, stirring constantly until smooth and thickened. Stir in salt, pepper, Worcestershire sauce, mushrooms and sherry. Preheat oven to 375 degrees F. and butter a 1½ quart casserole. Spread meat pieces and almonds over beans in casserole. Pour sauce over all. Sprinkle with cheese. Bake for 20 minutes. Cheese should be golden and bubbly.

The Landing

Cream Of Broccoli Soup

 Leaf 'N' Ladle

Serves: 10-12

2 tablespoons	butter, melted
1 medium	onion, chopped
½ cup	butter, melted
½ cup	flour
1 quart	Half and Half
1 quart	fresh chicken stock or chicken bouillon
1 pound	fresh broccoli, chopped
2 cups	carrots, julienned
	salt and pepper to taste
1 cup	heavy cream
½ teaspoon	nutmeg

Sauté onions in 2 tablespoons butter. Set aside. Cook butter and flour over medium heat for 3-5 minutes. Add the Half and Half slowly, stirring with a whisk. Add chicken stock and simmer for 20 minutes. Add broccoli, carrots and onions. Cook over low heat about 20-25 minutes or until flavors are blended and carrots are tender. Add salt and pepper to taste. Add heavy cream and nutmeg just before serving.

Leaf 'N' Ladle

Raspberry Sabayon Glacé

6	egg yolks
5 ounces	sugar, granulated
pinch	salt
1 teaspoon	heavy cream
½ cup	vanilla
6 ounces	white wine, medium dry
	Chambord raspberry liquor

Using an electric mixer on high speed, beat the first three ingredients until stiff and slightly white. Then, in a separate container from above, use medium heat to bring the cream, vanilla, wine and Chambord mixture to a simmer (do not boil). Place mixer on low speed while pouring the heated mixture into beaten egg yolks and sugar. Transfer combined ingredients to double boiler and stir (do not beat) constantly with a wisk until mixture thickens to whipped cream consistancy. Chill three hours in refrigerator. In a separate container, whip two cups of heavy cream, then fold whipped cream into main mixture. Place into individual serving containers, cover and allow to chill one hour in refrigerator (can remain overnight).

Top with fresh raspberries just prior to serving. Alternative toppings are blackberries or kiwi fruit.

Shangri-la

Shrimp Georgiades

2 cloves	fresh garlic, peeled and sliced
4	green onions, sliced
2 small	yellow onions, peeled and chopped
	olive oil, enough to cover bottom of frying pan
½ ounce	sherry wine
2 whole	ripe tomatoes, peeled and diced
	oregano
	salt
	pepper
	granulated garlic
2 dozen	shrimp, peeled and deveined
1 cup	Feta cheese, crumbled

Using an 11 inch frying pan, sauté sliced garlic and onions in olive oil until clear. Add sherry wine and tomatoes and sauté a few minutes longer until it starts to bubble. Add dry seasonings to taste and stir. Add shrimp and cook for 7 minutes or until shrimp turns red in color. Add Feta cheese and simmer until it begins to melt. Serve hot.

Liollio's

Pecan Pralines

Yield: 30 pieces

1½ cups	brown sugar
1½ cups	sugar, granulated
1 cup	evaporated milk
2 tablespoons	butter
2 cups	pecans, broken
1 teaspoon	vanilla

Cook sugars and evaporated milk until soft ball forms in cold water. Remove from heat and add butter. Beat until creamy. Add pecans and vanilla. Drop onto waxed paper.

Los Pancho's

Primavera Fettuccine

4	eggs
¼ cup	Half and Half
2 tablespoons	vegetable oil
½ cup	mushrooms, sliced
½ cup	carrots, sliced
½ cup	cauliflower, sliced
½ cup	broccoli, sliced
½ cup	onion, sliced
1 clove	garlic, chopped
1 (16 ounce) package	fettuccine noodles
¼ cup	butter, cut in pieces
1 cup	Parmesan cheese, grated
	salt and pepper to taste

Beat eggs with cream in small bowl and set aside. Heat oil in large skillet. Add sliced vegetables and garlic to skillet and sauté until crisp and tender, about 6-8 minutes. Meanwhile, cook fettuccine al dente in large amount of boiling, salted water. Drain well. Transfer to large, warmed serving bowl. Add butter and toss lightly. Add egg and cream mixture and toss. Add vegetables and cheese and toss again. Season with salt and pepper. Serve hot. For a variation, omit the Parmesan cheese and top with Hollandaise, white or cheese sauce.

Mother Earth's

Steak Au Poivre

4 tablespoons	peppercorns, freshly cracked
2	New York strip steaks, 1-inch thick
2 tablespoons	oil
4 tablespoons	butter
½ cup	bourbon or cognac
½ cup	Burgundy wine
½ cup	water, mixed with 1 cube beef-flavored bouillon or 1 teaspoon beef base

One hour before time of cooking, crack fresh peppercorns in a napkin with a rolling pin or meat mallet. Press ¾ tablespoon peppercorns on each side of steak using palm of the hand. Let steaks sit at room temperature for 1 hour. Using a skillet, melt butter and oil, making sure not to burn the butter. Place steaks in pan and sear at high heat for 2 minutes on each side. Reduce heat to medium-high and cook another 2 minutes per side for rare steak. Increase time for desired doneness. Remove steaks. Pour bourbon or cognac in pan and light it with a match to burn glaze in bottom of pan. Add Burgundy and stir. Add beef base mixed with water. Cook until sauce reduces to half the original volume. For a spicier sauce, add more cracked pepper. Pour sauce over steak. Serve with fresh broccoli, baked potato and Cabernet Sauvignon.

Nautical Wheelers

NIKKO INN
Japanese Restaurant & Lounge

Beef Sukiyaki

Serves: 1

SUKIYAKI SAUCE

2 ounces	soy sauce
1½ ounces	water
1½ ounces	sake
¼ teaspoon	ajinomoto
3 tablespoons	sugar
1 ounce	onion, chopped
1 ounce	tofu
8 ounces	Chinese cabbage, chopped
2 ounces	yam noodles
2 ounces	green onions, chopped
2 ounces	fresh mushrooms, sliced
2 ounces	bamboo shoots
4 ounces	beef, sliced very thin (retain beef fat)

Combine soy sauce, water, sake, ajinomoto and sugar to make a sauce. Set aside. Heat heavy cast iron skillet on high heat. Coat insides of pan with beef fat. Remove fat. Add sauce to pan. Add onion, tofu and cabbage, keeping vegetables separate in pan. Add noodles, green onions, mushrooms and bamboo shoots. Simmer 1 minute. Add beef. Separate thin slices of beef and mix into vegetables. Coat all pieces of beef and vegetables well with sauce. Cook until beef is done. Serve immediately.

Nikko Inn

The "Original" Seafood Gumbo

The *Original*
Seafood & Oyster House
Restaurant

Yield: 16 gallons

	liquid shortening
2 cups	gumbo filé
1½ cups	garlic salt
1 cup	salt
3½ cups	Louisiana hot sauce (not Tabasco)
2½ cups	Worcestershire sauce
13 jumbo	onions, diced
40 cups	canned peeled tomatoes, mashed
9 pounds	okra, sliced
15	bay leaves
4 gallons	water
6 cups	rice
10 pounds	shrimp, peeled and deveined
1 gallon	cut fish (amberjack)
2 gallons	water
1¼ pounds	chicken fry mix

Make a roux using a 12 quart pot. Cover the bottom lightly with liquid shortening. Add gumbo filé, garlic salt, salt, hot sauce, Worcestershire sauce and onions. Cook until onions are done or about 1 hour. In a separate pot cook tomatoes, okra and bay leaves until okra is done. In another pot, bring 4 gallons of water to a boil and add the rice. Lower heat and cook 10 minutes. Then add shrimp and fish, cooking another 10 minutes. After roux has thickened, take the 2 gallons of water and mix with the chicken fry mix. Mix until chicken fry is completely dissolved, using warm water. Pour this mixture into roux and stir until like a paste. Add the okra and tomato mixture and the rice and seafood mixture to the roux.

**The Original
Seafood & Oyster House
Restaurant**

Burgundy Mushrooms

Serves: 4-6

Great with steak.

1 pound	mushrooms
6 cups	beef-flavored bouillon
1 cup	Burgundy wine
1 tablespoon	garlic powder

Clean mushrooms. Bring all ingredients to a boil in a large saucepan and reduce to simmer. Simmer about 30 minutes or until tender.

**Pandora's Steak House
& Lounge**

Crabmeat Louisianne

1 stick	butter, melted
1 cup	green onions, chopped
1 teaspoon	parsley
1 teaspoon	cayenne
1½ teaspoons	black pepper
2 tablespoons	lemon juice
⅓ teaspoon	garlic powder
	salt to taste
1⅓ cups	toasted almonds
1⅓ cups	lump crabmeat

Sauté all ingredients except almonds and crabmeat. Fold in crabmeat and almonds and stir gently until hot. Serve over steamed saffron rice.

Paradise Cafe

Perri's Italian Restaurant

Marinated Mushrooms
Da Vinci

Serves: 14

2 pounds	fresh mushrooms
1½ ounces	celery hearts and leaves, finely chopped
1½ ounces	green onions, finely chopped
1½ ounces	white onions, finely chopped
1 tablespoon	parsley, chopped
2 teaspoons	monosodium glutamate
½ teaspoon	black pepper
½ teaspoon	oregano
½ teaspoon	sweet basil
2 tablespoons	lemon juice, freshly squeezed
1½ cups	red wine vinegar
5 cups	vegetable oil
2 cups	water
½ ounce	fresh garlic, chopped
2 teaspoons	salt

Combine all ingredients in a 1 gallon jar. Cover and shake the jar several times to blend ingredients thoroughly. Store in refrigerator for 2 days, shaking periodically to minimize separation. After 2 days, drain liquid; arrange on a bed of lettuce and garnish.

Perri's Italian Restaurant

Ponchartrain Sauce

1 pound	margarine, melted
1 quart	green pepper, shredded with a knife
1 quart	onion, shredded with a knife
1 bunch	green onions, chopped
½ cup	lemon juice
2 tablespoons	Worcestershire sauce
3	bay leaves
1 teaspoon	black pepper
½ cup	chicken base
1 tablespoon	Tabasco sauce (should be fairly hot)
1 pint	mushrooms, sliced
2 pounds	shrimp, peeled and deveined
½ cup	pimento, chopped
1 cup	sherry
	cornstarch to thicken

Combine and sauté margarine, green pepper, onions, lemon juice, Worcestershire sauce, bay leaves, pepper, chicken base and Tabasco sauce until vegetables begin to soften. Add mushrooms and sauté until they soften; add shrimp and cook to a boil. Add pimento and sherry. Add cornstarch to thicken; reduce heat. Serve over poached or sautéed fish.

Pier 98

Sand Flea

Oysters Sandflea

oysters
jalapeño cheese
seasoned salt

Place fresh oysters on the half-shell on a cookie sheet or oven-proof pan. Broil until edges begin to curl. Remove from oven and season each oyster with seasoned salt and jalapeño cheese. Place under broiler until cheese melts. May also be prepared in a microwave.

Sandflea

Seagull

Seviche

2 pounds small	shrimp
1 cup	catsup
½ cup	lemon juice
1 tablespoon	leaf oregano
1 small	purple onion, slivered
1 medium	bell pepper, slivered
	Tabasco sauce to taste
	salt to taste

Boil shrimp until pink. Peel and set aside. Mix remaining ingredients together in a large glass bowl or gallon jar. Add shrimp and toss well. If more sauce is needed, add 1 part lemon to 3 parts catsup until desired amount of sauce is prepared. Refrigerate for at least 12 hours or overnight. Serve with salty crackers.

Seagull

Seaside Shrimp

SEASIDE

Serves: 4

½ cup	olive oil
½ cup	corn oil
1 clove	garlic, crushed
1 tablespoon	red pepper, crushed
1 tablespoon	rosemary, crushed
½ teaspoon	basil
2½ to 3 pounds	shrimp (in the shell with heads off)
	salt
	pepper
	fresh lemon juice

Combine oils, garlic, red pepper, rosemary and basil to make a marinade for the shrimp. Refrigerate and let sit for 6 hours but is improved if it sits for 24 hours. Sauté shrimp in the marinade at low temperature in a heavy skillet for 5-6 minutes. Do not overcook. Season with salt, black pepper and fresh lemon juice. Serve over toasted French bread.

Snapper Seasons

Seaside Grill

Serves: 8

8 (7 ounce) pieces	red snapper
¾ cup	olive oil
3 teaspoons	lemon juice
½ teaspoon	dry mustard
1 tablespoon	fresh dill
1 tablespoon	dry dill weed
½ clove	garlic, crushed
⅓ cup	fresh cucumber, peeled and diced
⅓ cup	shrimp, diced (peeled and deveined)

Cut each piece of snapper into 3 pieces. Broil snapper for 8 minutes. Sauté broiled snapper with all other ingredients over high flame for 3 minutes. Arrange 3 pieces of fish per plate; spoon sauté mixture over top of fish. Garnish with yellow squash and zucchini.

The Seasons Restaurant at Bluewater Bay Resort

Chicken And Shrimp Chop Suey

Shangri-La

Serves: 4

2 tablespoons	celery, chopped
2 tablespoons	bamboo shoots, chopped
2 tablespoons	carrots, chopped
2 tablespoons	mushrooms, halved
½ cup	Chinese cabbage, shredded
½ cup	bean sprouts
½ cup	chicken breasts, sliced in thin strips
½ cup medium	shrimp, peeled and deveined
½ cup	vegetable oil
½ teaspoon	monosodium glutamate
1 tablespoon	soy sauce
1 tablespoon	oyster sauce
½ cup	water
1 tablespoon	cornstarch, mixed with 1 tablespoon water
	cooked rice

Soak vegetables in water for 15 minutes and drain. Heat oil in medium saucepan over medium heat. Fry shrimp and chicken, sprinkling with the monosodium glutamate, soy sauce and oyster sauce and stirring until meat is barely cooked (chicken color changes to white). Add water; cover and simmer for 5 minutes. Slowly add cornstarch, stirring until thickened. Serve with rice.

Shangri-La

Shrimp Bisque

Yield: 15 cups

4½ pounds	shrimp, peeled and poached
1 cup + 2 tablespoons	butter
6 tablespoons	green onions (grated, tops and all)
2 quarts + 1 cup	warm milk
3 cups	cream
1 cup	sherry
6 tablespoons	parsley, chopped
	salt
	pepper
	paprika
	nutmeg

Chop shrimp in processor or by hand. Sauté shrimp, butter and onion until shrimp is pink. Do not overcook. Add to warm milk and cream. Add sherry and parsley and seasonings to taste. Serve when warm. Do not boil. For an even richer bisque, use Half and Half and cream. For a variation, use lobster.

The Sound

Fish Chowder

8 pounds	snapper, grouper, scamp or red fish (whole)
	salt and white pepper
6 large	potatoes, peeled
16	scallions, chopped
3	fresh celery leaves, chopped
6 medium	tomatoes, chopped
3 medium	green peppers, chopped
1½ cups	tomato paste
2 tablespoons	Worcestershire sauce
16	peppercorns
½ cup	parsley, minced
2 teaspoons	basil
2 teaspoons	oregano
4 large	bay leaves
3	lemons (unpeeled and unsliced)
2½ cups	red wine
6 slices	bacon
10 tablespoons	flour
3 large	onions, chopped
4 cloves	garlic, chopped
8 cups	tomatoes, canned

Cut fish crosswise into steaks about 1¼ inches thick. Sprinkle steaks with salt and pepper and set aside. Boil up fish heads and backbones to yield 4 gallons of stock. Cut potatoes into 1 inch cubes. Set aside. Place scallions, celery leaves, fresh tomatoes and green peppers in a large bowl and add tomato paste, Worcestershire sauce, peppercorns, herbs, lemons and 1 cup of the wine. Set aside. Heat a cast iron pot (6-8 quarts) or a deep iron Dutch oven. Put in the bacon slices and heat until all fat is extracted and the bacon is crisp. Lift out bacon and pat dry; crumble and set aside. Gradually sprinkle the flour into the fat, stirring all the time. Cook, stirring until roux is the color of strong coffee with cream, being careful not to scorch it. Add chopped onion and garlic and continue to cook until onion is translucent but not browned. Keep stirring not letting anything scorch. Add canned tomatoes and heat, stirring until well mixed with the roux. Add boiling stock to within 4 inches of top of pot. Add the bowl of chopped ingredients and seasonings and return the bacon crumbs. Bring to a boil; reduce to simmer and cover. Let mixture simmer for 2-3 hours. Stir occasionally and add a little hot water if liquid is reduced too much. Add cubed potatoes and cook for a few minutes. Add fish steaks and cook until potatoes and fish are just done (the potatoes still somewhat crisp and the fish in whole pieces). Add remaining wine.

Scamp À La Docie

Serves: 8

8 (10 ounce)	scamp filets
3 medium	bell peppers, thinly sliced
3 medium	tomatoes, thinly sliced
1 large	onion, thinly sliced
½ cup	olive oil
¼ cup	lemon juice
1 tablespoon	cornstarch
	salt and pepper to taste

Sauté peppers, tomatoes and onions in olive oil until tender. Add lemon juice. Mix cornstarch with juices from the pan, stirring mixture to make a thin gravy. Add salt and pepper to taste. Serve over cooked fish.

The Staff Restaurant

Molded Spinach Salad

Serves: 6

1 (3 ounce) package	lemon flavored gelatin
1 ½ tablespoons	vinegar
½ cup	mayonnaise
¼ teaspoon	salt
⅓ cup	celery, chopped
1 tablespoon	onion, minced
1 cup	chopped frozen spinach, thawed and drained
¾ cup	cottage cheese

Dissolve gelatin in ¾ cup of boiling water. Add 1 cup cold water. Add vinegar, mayonnaise and salt. Put in a freezer tray and chill until firm 1 inch around the sides of the tray. Remove from freezer and beat until fluffy. Add onion, celery, spinach and cottage cheese. Fill a 1 quart mold and chill until firm.

Upper Crust

Children's

Children's Section

Razzle Dazzle Soda

Serves: 4

1 (10 ounce) package	frozen strawberries, thawed
3 cups	strawberry ice cream
2 (12 ounce) cans	cream soda
	whipped cream or topping
4 whole	fresh strawberries

Mash thawed strawberries. Add 1 cup ice cream and ½ cup soda, stirring well. Spoon mixture into four (14 ounce) soda glasses. Top with remaining ice cream and fill glasses with remaining soda. Garnish each with whipped cream and a strawberry.

Nancy Jones

Sunshine Punch

Serves: 8-10

1 (3 ounce) package	flavored gelatin
1 (48 ounce) can	pineapple juice, unsweetened
1 juice can	water
1 teaspoon	almond extract
1 teaspoon	lemon juice
1½ cups	sugar

Mix gelatin according to directions with sugar. Add remaining ingredients and freeze. Remove from freezer and let stand at room temperature 3-4 hours before serving.

Becky Ratcliff

Banana Blender Breakfast

Serves: 1

1	banana
1 cup	milk
2	egg yolks
½ teaspoon	vanilla
1 tablespoon	honey (optional)

Combine all ingredients in blender and blend until smooth.

Carole Gordon

Punch For A Bunch

Serves: 50

Serve in a washtub or an insulated cooler; use the drain hole for a kid-proof spout.

3 (12 ounce) cans	frozen orange juice, unsweetened
1 (18 ounce) can	pineapple juice, unsweetened
1 (46 ounce) can	apple juice, unsweetened

Mix orange juice according to directions. Combine with other juices. No sugar needed.

Bill Kilpatrick

Ants On A Log

celery stalks
peanut butter
raisins

Cut and wash celery stalks. Spread peanut butter inside each stalk. Top with raisins.

Betty Sahm

Pizza Muffins

Serves: 1

English muffin
butter
tomato sauce
oregano (powdered)
American cheese, shredded
Parmesan cheese, grated

Split and butter muffins. Toast muffin under broiler. Spread with tomato sauce. Add a dash of oregano, shredded cheese and a dash of Parmesan cheese. Toast under broiler until cheese melts.

Lindsay Maney

Rag Doll Salad

Serves: 1

1	peach half (canned)
4 small	celery sticks
1 large	marshmallow
6	raisins
2 tablespoons	yellow cheese, shredded
1	maraschino cherry
1 large	lettuce leaf

Place peach half for body on salad plate. Arrange celery for arms and legs. Use marshmallow for head; raisins for eyes, nose, shoes and buttons; and a small piece of the cherry for the mouth. Arrange cheese around marshmallow for hair. Add a skirt of leaf lettuce to complete the salad.

Patty Etheredge

285

Candle Salad

Serves: 4

4	lettuce leaves, washed
4 slices	pineapple
2	bananas
4	cherries

Place lettuce and pineapple slices on 4 salad plates. Peel and cut the bananas in half, crosswise. Stand each inside a pineapple slice and top with a cherry.

Ryland Parker

Animal Sandwich Cookies

Serves: 4

Fun for the children!

1/3 cup	peanut butter
1/4 cup	cream cheese, softened
2 tablespoons	honey
	bread

Combine peanut butter, cream cheese and honey in mixing bowl. Stir until well-blended. Trim crust from bread. Cut into animal shapes using cookie cutters. Spread peanut butter on half the bread animals and top with a matching animal.

Rhonda Mead

Monsters

Yield: 2 sandwiches

Let your child do this alone.

	peanut butter
2 slices	bread
	cheese spread in push-button cans
	peanuts

Spread peanut butter on bread slices. Make faces with the cheese spread. Decorate with peanuts. May substitute sandwich meat for peanut butter.

Barbara Born's Kindergarten Class

Easy Hamburger Quiche

Serves: 6-8

½ pound	ground beef
½ cup	mayonnaise
½ cup	milk
2	eggs
1 tablespoon	cornstarch
1½ cups	Cheddar cheese, grated
¼ cup	green onions, sliced
dash	pepper
1 (9 inch)	pastry shell, unbaked

Brown meat in skillet over medium heat. Drain fat. Blend mayonnaise, milk, eggs and cornstarch until smooth. Stir in meat, cheese, onions and pepper. Pour into pastry shell. Bake at 350 degrees F. for 35-40 minutes or until golden brown on top. Knife inserted in center should come out clean.

Nancy Jones

287

Rudolph Sandwiches

Kids love it!

bread
peanut butter
jelly
raisins
maraschino cherries
pretzels, broken in half

Make a peanut butter and jelly sandwich. Cut it diagonally. Place 2 raisins on the wide side of the bread for eyes, a cherry on the tip of the triangle for the nose and pretzels for the antlers. (Use peanut butter to "glue" the trimmings.)

Barbara Starling

Crunchy Date Delights   Yield: 3 dozen

1 (8 ounce) box	dates, chopped
½ cup	butter
1 cup	sugar
2½ cups	rice cereal
1¼ teaspoons	vanilla
1 cup	pecans, walnuts or almonds, chopped
	powdered sugar
	coconut (optional)

Combine dates, butter and sugar in a medium saucepan over medium heat for 5-8 minutes. Remove from heat and add cereal, vanilla and nuts. Roll into small balls; then roll in powdered sugar or mixture of powdered sugar and coconut.

Charlene Caluda

I Can't Believe
It's A Cookie

1 cup	crunchy peanut butter
1 cup	sugar
1	egg, beaten
1 teaspoon	vanilla

Combine all ingredients, mixing well. Roll dough into balls, using about 1 teaspoon dough for each ball. Place on ungreased cookie sheet about 1 inch apart. Press with bottom of glass. Bake at 350 degrees F. for 10 minutes. Cool before removing from cookie sheet.

Dana Dee Davis

Jell-O Fun Balls
Serves: 10-12

Fun at Christmas with red and green.

3½ ounces	coconut
¾ cup	condensed milk
1 cup	pecans
1 (3 ounce) package	flavored gelatin

Mix all ingredients together and chill overnight. The next day, form into balls and roll in sugar.

Carole Gordon

No Bake
Peanut Butter Squares
Yield: 32 squares

¼ cup	butter
1 (10½ ounce) bag	miniature marshmallows
½ cup	peanut butter
5 cups	rice cereal

Melt butter, marshmallows and peanut butter over low heat. Stir in cereal. Grease a 9 x 13 inch pan with butter and press mixture into pan. Cut into squares.

Betty Sahm

Cowboy Cookies

Yield: 4 dozen

1 cup	granulated sugar
1 cup	dark brown sugar
1 cup	shortening
2	eggs
2 cups	flour
½ teaspoon	baking powder
1 teaspoon	baking soda
½ teaspoon	salt
1 teaspoon	vanilla
2¾ cups	quick oats
12 ounces	semi-sweet chocolate morsels

Mix all ingredients well. Dough should be dry. Drop rounded teaspoonfuls on ungreased cookie sheet. Bake at 325 degrees F. for 8-10 minutes. Add crunch to this chewy cookie with 1 cup chopped pecans.

Jenny Brand

Painted Cookies

1	egg yolk
¼ teaspoon	water
	food coloring
	sugar cookies

Blend egg yolk and water. Divide mixture among several custard cups. Add several drops of food coloring to each cup. Using small water color brushes, paint designs on sugar cookies. (Slice-and-bake cookies are great for this.) If paint thickens, add a few drops of water. Bake according to directions.

Sarah Maney

Strawberry Jell-O Cake   *Serves: 8*

For a variation use peach gelatin and fresh peaches.

1 box	white cake mix
1 (3 ounce) box	strawberry gelatin
¾ cup	salad oil
4	eggs
1 cup	strawberries
½ cup	butter, softened
1 (16 ounce) box	confectioners sugar
½ cup	strawberries

Beat cake mix, gelatin, oil and eggs for 3 minutes at high speed. Add strawberries and beat 1 minute. Pour into oiled tube pan. Bake at 350 degrees F. for 40-45 minutes. Allow cake to cool in pan for 10 minutes; remove to cool on wire rack.

To make frosting, cream softened butter and 1 cup powdered sugar. Add berries and remaining sugar alternately. Spread on cooled cake.

Mona Kilpatrick

Raisin-Peanut Popcorn Balls   *Yield: 8-10 balls*

5 cups	popcorn, popped
1 cup	raisins
1 cup	salted peanuts
¾ cup	light brown sugar, packed
⅔ cup	granulated sugar
½ cup	water
⅓ cup	light corn syrup
½ teaspoon	vanilla

Combine popcorn, raisins and peanuts in a large bowl. Mix both sugars, water and corn syrup. Bring to a boil without stirring. Remove from heat and add vanilla. Pour syrup over popcorn mixture. Mix well with wooden spoon. Butter hands and form quickly into balls.

Jewel Howard

291

Pumpkin Cupcakes
Yield: 36 cupcakes

A nutritious snack!

3 cups	sugar
1 cup	salad oil
4	eggs
2 cups	pumpkin
3½ cups	flour
2 teaspoons	baking soda
1 teaspoon	salt
1 teaspoon	cinnamon
1 teaspoon	nutmeg
½ teaspoon	ground cloves
⅔ cup	water
1 cup	nuts or raisins

Cream sugar and oil together. Add eggs and pumpkin, mixing well. Sift together dry ingredients and add them to the pumpkin mixture alternately with water. Pour into 36 lined cupcake tins and bake at 350 degrees F. for 30-40 minutes.

Jennifer Taylor

Banana-Chocolate Chip Muffins
Serves: 8-10

A mid-morning snack or a lunch box treat.

1 package	banana nut bread or cake mix
½ to 1 cup	ripe bananas, mashed
1 cup	semi-sweet chocolate chips

Prepare cake mix according to directions. Stir in mashed bananas and chocolate chips. Pour into greased muffin tins. Bake at 350 degrees F. for 15-18 minutes.

Debra L. Lackey

Phony Ice Cream
Serves: 12

Make Phony Flower Pots by decorating with lollipops and green gum drops.

1 box	cake mix
12	ice cream cups
	frosting mix (any flavor)
12	cherries

Prepare cake mix according to package directions. Spoon batter into ice cream cups to almost full. Place on shallow pan and bake according to package directions for cupcakes. When cool, frost and decorate to look like ice cream with a cherry on top. May use nuts, candies, coconut, colored sugars or chocolate sprinkles for decorations.

Ashley Lynne Doolin

Fun Pops

1 (10½ ounce) bag	marshmallows
1 (12 ounce) package	chocolate chips
	toothpicks
	assorted decorations
	(raisins, coconut, nuts, gumdrops)

Melt chocolate chips over low heat. Dip marshmallows on a toothpick into melted chocolate. Decorate and eat immediately or place on wax paper.

David Sahm

Finger Jell-O

Yield: 100 squares

Great for toddlers or to pack in a lunch box.

4 envelopes	unflavored gelatin
3 (3 ounce) packages	gelatin, any flavor
4 cups	boiling water

Combine gelatins in a large bowl. Add boiling water and stir until completely dissolved. Pour into a 13 x 9-inch pan and chill until firm. Cut into squares. This may be picked up and eaten with fingers.

Cathy Colwell

Molded Popcorn Centerpiece

Yield: 1 centerpiece

For special holidays, fill the ring with Christmas ornaments, a plastic Halloween pumpkin or plastic Easter eggs.

7 cups	popcorn, popped
½ cup	brown sugar, packed
¼ cup	margarine
2 tablespoons	light corn syrup
¼ teaspoon	salt
¼ teaspoon	baking soda

Generously grease a ring mold. Heat together brown sugar, margarine, syrup and salt until bubbly around edges of the pan, stirring constantly. Cook without stirring for 4 minutes. Remove from heat and stir in baking soda. This will make the mixture foam. Drizzle mixture over popped corn in a large bowl. Stir until the corn is well-coated. Press popcorn into ring mold. Let stand to dry for 1 hour. Prior to serving, run spatula around edges of mold. Turn mold on its side and hit it sharply against a counter top. Place popcorn ring on a plate to serve.

Sally Chambless

Pretty Pretzels

Practice makes perfect but they always taste good!

1 package	dry yeast
½ cup	warm water
1	egg, separated
¼ cup	sugar
¼ cup	margarine
1 cup	milk
1 teaspoon	salt
5 cups	flour
	coarse salt
	mustard

Dissolve yeast in warm water. Mix egg yolk, sugar, margarine and milk into yeast. Add salt and enough flour to make a stiff dough. Knead dough on a floured surface for 5 minutes. Let rise 1 hour. Roll dough out; cut into 1 inch wide strips and twist into a rope. Shape the rope into designs — fish, snakes, snails, people, hearts and butterflies. Be imaginative. Beat 1 tablespoon of water into egg white. Brush on pretzel; sprinkle with salt and bake at 425 degrees F. for 15-20 minutes (until golden brown). Serve with mustard.

Ashley Lynne Doolin

Turtles

Parental guidance suggested.

> pecan pieces
> caramels
> chocolate chips

Place 5 pieces of pecans on a greased cookie sheet. Top each with a caramel. Bake at 350 degrees for 4-6 minutes. Press each caramel with a buttered spatula. Melt some chocolate chips and frost each turtle. Cool and eat.

Betty Sahm

Bubble Soap   *Yield: 1 quart*

8 tablespoons	dishwashing liquid
1 quart	water

Fill quart bottle and use for children's bath. May also be used to blow bubbles.

Jenny Brand

Play Dough   *Yield: 1 quart*

Water soluble and easy to clean up!

2 cups	flour
1 cup	salt
2 cups	water
2 tablespoons	cooking oil
4 tablespoons	cream of tartar
	food coloring

Mix dry ingredients in a large saucepan. Add oil and water until smooth. Cook over medium heat, stirring until mixture leaves the side of the pan. Turn out on waxed paper and knead in food coloring. Keep in an airtight container.

Netta Holley

Gifts

Gifts

Christmas Liqueur

A pretty red color. Place in a clear bottle and tie with green ribbon for an attractive Christmas gift for friends.

2 cups	sugar
2 cups	cranberries, crushed
2 cups	vodka

Combine all ingredients in a large, covered jar and place in a dark, cool place for 3 weeks. Stir occasionally. Strain through cheesecloth and pour into decorative decanters.

Linda Carr

Orange Brandy

Serve after a holiday dinner. Give guests a gift bottle that has a pretty orange ribbon attached!

1 bottle	brandy
4	navel oranges
1 1/3 cups	honey

Strip peel from oranges and remove as much white pulp from peel as possible. Marinate orange peel in brandy at room temperature for 4 weeks. Remove orange peel and pour in honey. Stir until honey is dissolved. Let stand 4 to 6 days. Decant and bottle. Brandy will reach its peak flavor in about 4 weeks.

Nancy Kruzek

Kahlua

Add a jigger to your coffee for a spicy after-dinner drink. Stir with a cinnamon stick.

2 cups	drip ground coffee
2½ cups	cold water
3 cups	sugar
2 cups	water
2 cups	190 proof grain alcohol
2 ounces	vanilla

Bring coffee and water to a boil; cover and simmer for 40 minutes. Strain in a cheesecloth. Set aside. Boil sugar in water for 5 minutes. Add to strained coffee, stirring slowly. Let cool. Mix in grain alcohol and vanilla.

Marianne Calvin

Hot Chocolate Mix   *Yield: 1-gallon*

So easy that children can make this, pour into decorative tins and give to their friends. Be sure to include directions for serving when giving as gifts.

1 (8 quart) box	powdered milk
1 (6 ounce) jar	non-dairy creamer
1 pound	instant chocolate mix
2 cups	powdered sugar

Sift all ingredients together and store in an airtight container. To serve, combine ½ cup mix to ½ cup boiling water.

Martha Kilpatrick

Orange-Coated Walnuts

Add these as a personal touch to your gift baskets of Florida oranges.

⅓ cup	orange juice concentrate
1 teaspoon	lemon extract
1 cup	sugar
1 tablespoon	butter
2½ cups	walnuts

Combine orange juice concentrate, lemon extract, sugar and butter in a saucepan. Heat until mixture becomes creamy and loses sugary look. Stir constantly. Mix in walnuts and pour onto wax paper. Separate walnuts and cool.

Linda Scoville

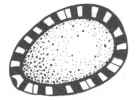

Spicy Sugared Nuts

These can be given in a candy dish or in a decorative tin.

2 cups	pecans or walnuts
1 tablespoon	egg white
¼ cup	sugar
1 tablespoon	cinnamon

Mix nuts with egg white and stir until sticky. Mix cinnamon with sugar and sprinkle on nuts. Stir to coat and bake on a cookie sheet at 300 degrees F. for 30 minutes.

Kathy Wile

Herbed Boursin Cheese

For gift-giving, use a decorative ceramic jelly jar or a pretty crock.

3 (8 ounce) packages	cream cheese
3 cloves	garlic, crushed
2 tablespoons	vermouth
2 teaspoons	dried parsley, minced
¾ teaspoon	salt
½ teaspoon	dried basil
¼ teaspoon	dried tarragon
¼ teaspoon	sage
¼ teaspoon	white pepper

Mix all ingredients in food processor or blender. Place in crock at least 1 day before serving.

Margie Hooker

Christmas Chinese Chews

Pretty to serve or pretty to give!

¾ cup	sugar
2 eggs	beaten together
1 teaspoon	cinnamon
1 teaspoon	nutmeg
1 teaspoon	allspice
1 teaspoon	vanilla
3 heaping tablespoons	flour
1 (8 ounce) box	dates, chopped
1 cup	pecans or walnuts, chopped
	red or green maraschino cherries

Combine all ingredients in a bowl. Pour mixture into 22 miniature foil baking cups inside miniature muffin pans. Garnish with half a cherry on top of each mixture in foil cup. Bake at 350 degrees F. for 30 minutes. Leave muffin in foil containers to serve or place in a gift tin.

Virginia Glynn Barr

Nut Tea Cakes

The recipe for these dainty tea cakes or cookies comes from a December 24, 1926, issue of **The Spray,** *the area's first newspaper. Printing of the weekly paper was done on a Washington hand press and a lever had to be pushed down to print each page. Copies of* **The Spray** *are on display at Camp Walton Schoolhouse, a one-room schoolhouse which has been historically restored by the Junior Service League and is open to the public.*

½ cup	butter
1 cup	light brown sugar
¼ cup	milk
2 eggs	beaten
2 cups	flour
2 teaspoons	baking powder
1 cup	nuts, chopped

Cream butter and sugar. Combine milk and eggs and add alternately to sugar mixture with dry ingredients that have been sifted together. Stir in nuts. Drop by teaspoonfuls onto an ungreased baking sheet. Bake at 350 degrees F. until brown.

Winn Shuler Crock

Easy to prepare. Make this ahead of time and store.

1 ½ pounds	Velveeta cheese
1 cup	unsalted butter
2 teaspoons	onion juice
1 (3 ounce) package	cream cheese
⅔ cup	horseradish
	red and yellow food color

Heat all ingredients in a double boiler until melted. Beat with electric mixer for 3 minutes. Add 2 drops red food color and 1 drop yellow food color to mixture. Place in a deep dish or crock and cool in refrigerator. Serve with crackers.

Margie Hooker

Toffee Brickle

Be sure to include this when making your Christmas goodies. Children love to help by breaking the toffee into pieces.

1 cup	butter
1 cup	sugar
1 teaspoon	vanilla
2 teaspoons	water
	chocolate chips
	chopped nuts

Cook first 4 ingredients in a medium saucepan on medium-high heat. Cook slowly. When mixture begins to bubble and turn brown, remove from heat and spread evenly on a buttered cookie sheet. Do this quickly as candy will harden. Sprinkle chocolate chips over the top. When chips begin to melt, spread over the candy with a spatula. Sprinkle with chopped nuts. Let cool and harden; then break into pieces.

Suzanne Seemann

Potato Candy

An unusual combination — a pleasing surprise!

¼ cup	mashed potatoes
1 teaspoon	vanilla
3 cups	powdered sugar
	chunky peanut butter

Combine first 3 ingredients. Add more powdered sugar if necessary and mix until stiff enough to roll out. Roll into a rectangle; spread top with peanut butter and roll as for jellyroll. Chill; slice and serve.

Janice Prescott

Nine Bean Soup

A novel idea when many gifts are needed. It would be attractive to layer the beans in 9 clear jars. Tie a pretty ribbon around the jars and attach a wooden soup spoon. Or place mixture in clear plastic storage bags and give in a basket with 2 soup mugs.

2 cups	Nine Bean Soup Mix
8 cups	water
1 pound	ham, diced
1 large	onion, chopped
1 clove	garlic, minced
½ teaspoon	salt
1 (16 ounce) can	tomatoes, chopped, do not drain
1 (10 ounce) can	tomatoes and green chilies, chopped, do not drain

Rinse bean mix. Place in large Dutch oven; cover with water and let soak overnight. Drain. Add next 5 ingredients, cover and bring to a boil. Reduce heat and simmer for 1½ hours or until beans are tender. Add remaining ingredients and simmer for 30 minutes, stirring occasionally.

Nine Bean Soup Mix

1 pound	black beans, dried
1 pound	red beans, dried
1 pound	pinto beans, dried
1 pound	navy beans, dried
1 pound	great northern beans, dried
1 pound	lentils, dried
1 pound	split green peas, dried
1 pound	black-eyed peas, dried
1 pound	barley, dried

Mix all beans together. Divide bean mix into nine, 2-cup packages. Place in jars or bags with the recipe attached for Nine Bean Soup.

Barbara Smith

Crunchy Sweet Pickles   *Yield: 1 gallon*

1 gallon	sliced dill pickles
5 pounds	granulated sugar
1 quart	cider vinegar
1 (1½ ounce) box	pickling spice, tied in a cheesecloth bag
2 tablespoons	alum
Cloves (1 for each jar)	garlic

Drain dill pickles and transfer to a large bowl. Add enough boiling water to cover pickles. Add alum and let pickles stand overnight. Next day, drain pickles in a colander; do not rinse. In a large pot gently boil sugar, vinegar and pickling spice bag for 10 minutes. Add pickles to boiling mixture and bring to a boil again. Continue boiling for 12 minutes or until pickles turn clear. Lift out spice bag and let pickles and juice cool. Place a clove of garlic in each jar and fill with pickles and juice. These jars need not be sterile or sealed. For best flavor, store pickles for 2 weeks before giving as gifts.

Bertha Anderson

Granola

An excellent breakfast cereal or healthy snack. A treat for adults or children to receive as gifts.

½ cup	oil
1 cup	honey
5 cups	oatmeal
5 cups (1 cup each of any 5)	pecans, almonds, walnuts, raisins, coconut, wheat germ, mixed dried fruit or any 1 single dried fruit

Heat oil and honey until warm. Add all other ingredients. Spread in two 9 x 13 x 2 inch pans that are well-greased. Bake at 275 degrees F. for 1 hour or until brown. Stir every 20 minutes. Cool and store in airtight containers. Granola will become crunchy as it cools.

Ellyn Smith

Cream Cheese Coffee Braid

Freezes well. This recipe includes a treat for your family and three for friends.

1 cup	sour cream
½ cup	sugar
1 teaspoon	salt
½ cup	butter or margarine
½ cup	warm water
2 packages	yeast
2	eggs
4 cups	flour

FILLING

2 (8 ounce) packages	cream cheese
1	egg, beaten
2 teaspoons	vanilla
¾ cup	sugar
⅛ teaspoon	salt

GLAZE

2 cups	confectioners sugar
2 tablespoons	milk
2 teaspoons	vanilla

Scald sour cream and stir in sugar, salt and butter. Cool to lukewarm. Put warm water in a large, warm bowl and sprinkle in yeast and stir until dissolved. Add lukewarm sour cream mixture, eggs and mix well. Gradually stir in flour. Mix until well-blended. Cover in airtight container and refrigerate overnight. Divide dough into 4 equal parts. Work with 1 piece at a time and leave remaining pieces in the refrigerator. Roll into an 8 x 12 inch rectangle on a floured surface. Work fast because dough gets sticky. Prepare filling by mixing all ingredients. Spread filling on rectangle, using ¼ of the filling for each piece of dough. Roll as for a jellyroll. Pinch edges together and fold ends under slightly. Lay seam-side down on a greased, foil-covered cookie sheet. With scissors, cut each roll to resemble a braid. Alternate slashes from side to side about halfway through roll. Allow to rise until double in bulk, about 1 to 1½ hours. Bake at 350 degrees F. until light brown. Do not overcook. Remove from oven. Combine ingredients for glaze and drizzle over braid. This freezes well after baked. When ready to serve, thaw, reheat to warm and then add glaze.

Pam Williams

Pepper Jelly

Yield: 6 (½ pint) jars

Use your cross-stitch talents to make a pretty lid.

⅓ cup	jalapeño peppers, seeds removed, chopped
¾ cup	green pepper, finely chopped
1½ cups	cider vinegar
5½ cups	sugar
1 (6 ounce) bottle	pectin
	red or green food color

Process peppers and ½ cup vinegar in blender. Place peppers, remaining vinegar and sugar in a 5-quart saucepan and cook for 10 minutes. Add liquid pectin and boil for 1 minute. Strain. Cool for 10 minutes before putting into sterilized jelly jars.

Jackie Wright

Super Quick Jam

Great for last-minute gift-making during the holidays. Add a box of crackers and place in a pretty basket.

2 (10 ounce) packages	frozen berries in heavy syrup
1 cup	sugar

Combine berries and sugar and bring to a boil for 3 minutes. Do not drain. Cool slightly and pour into a sterilized, 12-ounce jelly jar. Does not need parafin to seal.

Virginia Glynn Barr

Index

311

313

Notes: